CW00411000

PROVE

FIFTH EDITION

by

STEWART CALLIGAN

LLB (Hons) (London)
Police Training School Director
Consultant on Police Matters

Author of:
The Custody Officer's Companion
    (co-author Paul Harper)
Policing Your Health
    (co-author Allan Charlesworth)
Taking Statements

Points to Prove

© Stewart Calligan 2000
ISBN 0 9533058 9 9

1st edition 1981, 2nd edition 1987, 3rd edition 1992
4th edition 1995, revised 4th edition 1997
Police Review Publishing Co Ltd

Fifth edition 2000
The New Police Bookshop

The New Police Bookshop
East Yorkshire, England, UK
(Law Authentication Work)

The New Police Bookshop
Surrey, England, UK
(Benson Publications)

Printed by Ashford Colour Press, Gosport, Hants

To order:

write to The New Police Bookshop
(East Yorkshire) PO Box 124, Goole DN14 7FH

Points to Prove (£13.00) The Custody Officer's Companion (16.50)
Policing Your Health (£10.00). All prices include postage and packing.
Cheques should be made payable to The New Police Bookshop.

PREFACE

'HOW TO USE THE LAW FOR PRACTITIONERS'

Simplicity is an aid to learning. With this statement in mind, I have chosen some 70 offences which can be found in the Police Summons and Charges lists and in the Magistrates' Court Sheets on most days of the week across the country.

Less common offences have not been included and this simplification has allowed me to spend more time on the type of offences you are likely to be concerned with.

The main problems encountered by people dealing with the detection, prosecution and the defence of offences are:

(A) What are the POINTS TO PROVE

(B) What do the points MEAN and

(C) How are the points PROVED or DISPROVED.

In some of the offences I have added a further heading of

(D) Supporting Evidence,

where other important matters are explained.

(A) Shows the correctly worded Summons or Charge, called **POINTS TO PROVE**. Each offence has been divided into its different elements, all of which have to be proved beyond all reasonable doubt for a successful prosecution.

(B) and **(C)** headings are drawn from legislation, case decisions and the normal practice of magistrates' courts.

It should be noted that the practice of some police officers to refer to case decisions as 'stated cases' is wrong. Only those cases stated from magistrates' courts to Crown courts or a High court on a point of law are 'stated cases'. It is safer, therefore, to refer to all as 'case decisions'.

Section 1 of the book deals with **Traffic**, section 2 with **Crime**, and section 3 with **Miscellaneous offences**. A **glossary** is provided for the traffic offences at the beginning of section 1 of the book.

THE FOURTH EDITION 1997

The fourth edition of 1997 covered the Criminal Justice and Public Order Act 1994 which produced several new offences, computer-held information, drugs, bilking, vehicle interference, counterfeit notes and coins and the new common assault charge.

THE FIFTH EDITION 2000

This new fifth edition contains all the relevant new legislation since 1997. Additional offences include being carried in or on a vehicle taken without the owner's consent; possessing dangerous drugs with intent to supply; offences under the Harassment Act 1997 and offences contrary to the Crime and Disorder Act 1998 viz - racially aggravated assaults, racially aggravated criminal damage, racially aggravated public order offences, and racially aggravated harassment.

Case law, statute law and procedures have been updated where necessary.

ACKNOWLEDGMENTS

I am greatly indebted to my wife Christine, Inspector Samantha Hellawell (LLB) and PC Jeremy Manning (BA) for their assistance with the compiling of this new edition.

Stewart Calligan
Yorkshire
February 2000

SUMMARY OF CONTENTS

CONTENTS

Offences listed chronologically

SECTION 1 - TRAFFIC
Traffic Glossary

SECTION 2 - CRIME

SECTION 3 - MISCELLANEOUS OFFENCES

Offences listed alphabetically

SECTION 1 - TRAFFIC

SECTION 2 - CRIME

SECTION 3 - MISCELLANEOUS OFFENCES

Section 1

Traffic

TRAFFIC GLOSSARY

DRIVE

The driver means the person having control of the direction and movement of the vehicle. Drive and driving are construed accordingly. In most of the authoritative cases the 'direction' is taken to be the steering and the 'movement' is taken to be the acceleration and braking.

Problems arise where a person is not fully in control of direction and movement. In *Ames v MacLeod* 1969 SC 1 and *R v McDonagh* [1974] RTR 372 a test was suggested, namely 'whether the person was in a substantial sense controlling the movement and direction of the car'. However, where this test is satisfied it may still not be conclusive proof that the person is 'driving' and it must be asked whether the person can be said to be 'driving' under the ordinary meaning of the word.

Examples which have been held to be 'driving' which do not readily fall within the above definition include:

(1) Where a girl was in the front passenger seat and leaned across to the driver's side, controlling the steering wheel with both hands, being within reach of the ignition and the hand brake. Her companion in the driver's seat who controlled the gears and the foot controls was also held to be driving.

(2) A person sitting behind the steering wheel being pushed by people outside the vehicle, if he is acting in conjunction with those people. The people pushing will aid and abet the driver.

(3) A learner driver sitting behind the steering wheel in a dual control vehicle is a driver although the qualified driver also has control of the vehicle and can also be said to be driving. A person supervising a learner driver in a single control vehicle may aid and abet the commission of an offence by the learner driver.

(4) A 'steersman' in a towed vehicle will be held to be 'driving' if the extent and degree of control could be said to correctly

describe 'driving' (*R v MacDonagh* [1974] RTR 372 and *McQuaid v Anderton* [1980] 3 All ER 540).

(5) Pedalling an auto-assisted bicycle without starting the engine has been held to be driving away.

(6) It is felt that a person propelling a motor cycle with his legs astride the cycle and his feet on the ground by 'paddling' it, would be driving.

MOTOR VEHICLE

A motor vehicle means a mechanically propelled vehicle intended or adapted for use on roads, section 185 (1) Road Traffic Act 1988.

A good illustration of 'intended' is found in the case of *Childs v Coghlan* (1968) 112 SJ 175 where a 30 ton earth mover which was made for use on construction sites and not roads was held to be a motor vehicle. As it was too large to be put on a lorry to be moved from site to site it had to travel on roads under its own power and was held to be intended to be used on roads.

Dumper trucks will normally not be classified as motor vehicles as they are not intended or adapted for use on roads. A Go-Kart is in a similar position, but both a dumper truck and a Go-Kart can become 'motor vehicles' if it can be proved that they have been adapted or intended for use on roads. Use of a vehicle at any particular time does not prove 'intended'. Proof of regular use on the road is usually called for. 'Adapted' means fit and apt for the purpose.

A test was laid down in 1987 as to whether a vehicle was **intended or adapted for use on roads**. It is whether a reasonable person, looking at the vehicle, and forming a view as to its general use, would say the vehicle might well be used on the road, *Chief Constable of Avon and Somerset v Fleming* [1987] 1 All ER 318.

Vehicles which are not to be treated as motor vehicles include pedestrian-controlled mechanically propelled vehicles and electrically assisted pedal cycles, section 189 Road Traffic Act 1988.

MECHANICALLY PROPELLED VEHICLE

As a start one should ask 'Is the vehicle constructed so that it can be mechanically propelled?' ie is there a mechanical means of propulsion other than 'person power' alone, such as pedalling a pedal cycle.

Mechanical propulsion presently ranges from steam, through the various petrols and oils to gas and electric, with nuclear or magnetic etc vehicles around the corner.

Helpful explanations can be found in the following cases:

(1) Don't ask whether the engine is in working order but ask, 'Is the vehicle constructed so that it can be mechanically propelled?' *R v Tashin* [1970] RTR 88.

(2) A temporary removal of the engine does not stop a vehicle being a 'mechanically propelled vehicle', *Newberry v Simmonds* [1961] 2 All ER 318.

(3) The opposite to 2. above was held where the vehicle was a broken down wreck in *Smart v Allan* [1962] 3 All ER 893.

(4) But see *Binks v Department* of the Environment (1975) 119 SJ 304 where a severely damaged car which the owner intended to repair, was held to be a mechanically propelled vehicle.

ROAD

Road is defined as any highway and any other road to which the public has access and includes bridges over which a road passes, section 192 Road Traffic Act 1988.

Highway is narrower in meaning than road and there must be some evidence of permanent dedication to the public. A court should take any map or plan etc into account when deliberating on the question of what is a highway.

Note. There is a rebuttable presumption that the highway includes everything between the fence or boundary wall etc, eg grass verges, footpaths and central reservations. But this is so only where the fence etc was erected with reference to the highway and would probably not apply where the fence was erected for some other reason (*A-G v Beynon* [1969] 2 All ER 263).

To amount to a **road**, the public must have legal and actual access. It must allow travellers to move from one place to another along a definable route with ascertainable edges. The question of whether a 'road' has been defined in law is a question of fact for the court to decide.

The main factor for a road is **public access**, but where to draw the line causes difficulty. It was held in *Cox v White* [1976] Crim LR 263 that a mere slight degree of access by the public is not sufficient.

General cases of interest concerning this definition include:

(1) *Harrison v Hill* 1932 SC (J) 13 where a road maintained by a farmer, leading from the public road to his farmhouse, was held to be a road. It was also used by people having no business at the farm although from time-to-time the farmer turned away people who were using it.

(2) In *Bugge v Taylor* (1940) 104 JP 467 the forecourt of a hotel was held to be a road. It was private property, but was used as a short cut from one street to another.

Note. For 'road' there must be a line of communication which can be described as a road and it is not sufficient merely to show vehicles have access, eg to a car-park.

(3) In *Cutter v Eagle Star insurance Company Ltd* [1998] it was held that a car park is not a road in the 'ordinary use of language', as a car park and road have separate characteristics and functions. A road enables movement to particular destinations and a car park enables stationary vehicles to stand and wait.

PUBLIC PLACE

'Public place' has been added to certain offences under the road traffic legislation to enlarge the use of the offences. Although not defined under the Road Traffic Act 1988, having regard to the spirit of the legislation, it is considered that that the definitions used in other Acts would apply.

These definitions include any place to which the public have access, whether on payment or otherwise, eg fields where the public can park for a race meeting or traction engine rally, footpaths or bridleways (unless the Act states otherwise: see section 22A (5) of the Road Traffic Act 1988), or anywhere where the public could lawfully be at risk from mechanically propelled vehicles.

It has been held that a 'public place' includes a multi-story car park when there was no barrier restricting entrance. *Bowman v DPP* [1991] RTR 263.

Conversely it has been held that the following were not public places - a public house car park outside licensing hours, or land open only to members of a proprietary club.

THAT YOU

'That you' prefaces most summons headings and merely means that the prosecution must be in a position to prove that the defendant in court is the person who they allege committed the offence.

It is very unlikely, although not unknown, that the defendant will deny being present etc, at the time of the offence.

He may still plead not guilty while admitting that he is the person concerned in the alleged offence.

When identity is in question, consider *R v Turnbull and Others* [1976] 3 All ER 549. Courts will normally look for the following points in disputed identity cases.

The eight points of *Turnbull*:
(1) How long did the witness observe the accused?
(2) How far away from the witness was the accused person?
(3) What were the lighting conditions at the time?
(4) Was the observation impeded in any way?
(5) Had the witness ever seen the accused before and, if so, how often?

(6) If the witness had only seen the accused occasionally, had the witness any special reason for remembering the accused?

(7) How long was the period of time between original observation and subsequent identification to the police?

(8) Was there any material discrepancy between the description of the accused given to the police by the witness when first seen and his actual appearance?

It is important that these points be addressed during the collection of evidence.

TRAILER

Trailer means vehicle drawn by a motor vehicle, section 185 Road Traffic Act 1988.

'Vehicle' was discussed in *Boxer v Snelling* [1972] RTR 472 where it was said that, in borderline cases, not only the construction or nature of the contrivance but also the circumstances of its use should be taken into account. A stall with wheels was held to be a vehicle in this case.

A motor vehicle which is being towed by another motor vehicle both remains a motor vehicle and also becomes a trailer. Therefore, such a towed motor vehicle can be subject to offences of using without tax or insurance or in contravention of the Construction and Use Regulations.

USE, CAUSE OR PERMIT

Use means 'to have the use of the motor vehicle on a road'.

The following cases will help to illustrate the variety of uses recognised by the courts:

(1) a vehicle placed on a road with the battery removed and incapable of being driven at all;

(2) when stationary on a road for loading or unloading;

(3) a vehicle being towed is apparently being 'used'.

Note. Where the offence in question gives alternatives of using, causing or permitting the use thereof, 'uses' is interpreted rather more strictly and restrictively than when an offence commences 'Did use', with no other alternatives. In such a restricted case, where there is a master-servant relationship it can usually be said that the master or employer 'uses' as well as the driver, being the servant or employee.

In *Green v Burnett* [1954] 3 All ER 273 it was held that an employer was guilty of 'using', as a vehicle with defective brakes was being used on his business. The Motor Vehicle (Construction and Use) Regulations generally impose an absolute liability even though an employer, as in this case, had no knowledge of the defect. In effect there is no necessity for *mens rea* or guilty knowledge in using offences.

In practice, 'use' is probably the easiest to prove and the hardest to disprove.

Cause means some express or positive mandate from the person 'causing' to the driver etc. *Mens rea* or guilty knowledge must be proved by the prosecution where a person is reported for an offence of 'causing'.

Permit means an express or implied permission and does not involve any order to take a vehicle on the roads. As with 'cause' *mens rea* must be proved.

VEHICLE

This is wider in meaning than 'motor vehicle' as 'vehicles' do not need to be mechanically propelled. Therefore, trailers and bicycles, as well as all kinds of mechanically propelled vehicles, are 'vehicles'.

A court will most likely look at the circumstances in which the article was used, as well as the construction, nature or function of it, in cases of difficulty.

1. CARELESS AND INCONSIDERATE DRIVING

Section 3 Road Traffic Act 1988 as amended by the Road Traffic Act 1991

(A) POINTS TO PROVE

1. That you 2. did drive 3. a certain mechanically propelled vehicle, namely a .... 4. on a road or other public place called .... 5. (a) without due care and attention or (b) without reasonable consideration for other persons using the road or public place.

(B) MEANING OF TERMS

■ **1. 'That you'**

Means the person driving the mechanically propelled vehicle (ie identity).

■ **2. 'did drive'** see Glossary

■ **3. 'a certain mechanically propelled vehicle, namely a ...'**

This phrase replaces 'motor vehicle' as defined in the Glossary. In the case of certain motor vehicles such as dumper trucks, the prosecution had to prove that they were intended or adapted for use on roads. All this offence now requires is that the vehicle in question is mechanically propelled, see Glossary.

■ **4. 'on a road or other public place called ....'**

The phrase 'other public place'. has been added. Although not defined it is considered that the definition used in other Acts will apply ie, 'Includes any place to which the public have access, whether on payment or otherwise'. Suffice it to say that the offence can now be committed in many more places than before. See Glossary.

■ **5. (a) 'without due care and attention'**

Means that the driver did not exercise that degree of care and attention which a reasonable and prudent driver would exercise in the circumstances. Each case will be decided on its own facts, *Tidy v Battman* [1934] 1 KB 319, CA.

■ 5. (b) 'without reasonable consideration for other persons using the road'.

Means that reasonable consideration was not shown, eg where a pedestrian is splashed by a car going through an obviously large puddle which could have been avoided, where headlights are left on full beam, so as to become a potential or an actual hazard, or when a driver changes lanes without reasonable consideration for other road users. In this case a driver may well have exercised due care and attention but the offence of driving without reasonable consideration may still be committed. Dangerous driving is usually reserved for intentional dangerous driving or where it can be proved the defendant was driving in such a way as to fall within the new definition of 'driving dangerously' in section 2A(1) to (4) of the Road Traffic Act 1988.

(C) USUAL METHODS OF PROVING THESE POINTS

■ 1. 'That you'

Cases are sometimes lost when the prosecution fails to identify the driver. This can be done simply by a witness being asked in court, 'Is the defendant the man you saw driving at the time of the offence?'

Problem areas include where two people share the controlling of the movement and direction of the vehicle. It was held in *Tyler v Whatmore* [1976] RTR 83 that two people can actually drive the same vehicle, at the same time. Here the front seat passenger leaned across the person sitting in the driver's seat and with both hands on the steering wheel, steered the car. The other person still controlled the propulsion.

Another problem arises where two people admit to being the driver of a vehicle and the police are unable to prove or disprove either statement. Offences such as wasting police time and perverting the course of justice could be considered, with the possibility of both being taken to court as drivers and letting the court decide.

■ 2. 'did drive'

Driving is usually proved by witness statements to the effect that they saw the defendant drive. In the absence of witnesses, only a confession on the part of the defendant or sufficient circumstantial evidence will substantiate the offence. Circumstantial evidence may include that the defendant was the only person with the car keys; he was seen getting out of the vehicle; he was seen going towards or getting in the vehicle and/or he said he was going to drive the vehicle.

■ 3. 'a certain mechanically propelled vehicle, namely a ....'

'Mechanically propelled vehicle' can be proved by a phrase in a witness statement to the effect, 'I saw him driving a Jaguar saloon motor car, registered number ....'

In borderline cases, such as broken down vehicles or power assisted pedal cycles, recourse must be had to the case law. See glossary. No doubt more case law will be forthcoming on the meaning of 'mechanically propelled'.

Expert evidence from a suitably qualified mechanical engineer may be necessary on a few occasions.

■ 4. 'on a road or other public place called ....'

'Road' is defined as 'any highway or any other road to which the public has access and includes bridges over which a road passes'. In problematical cases the following test might help - Has the general public access?

If 'Yes', then it is a road.

If 'No', then is a majority class or a minority class restricted from using it?

If only a minority class, then it will probably still be a road but if otherwise, generally not, unless it is a 'public place'. See glossary.

Where a road is shown on a 'definitive' map prepared under the Countryside Act 1968, Schedule 3, as a 'byway open to all traffic' this can be taken as conclusive evidence that the public have access.

However, where a right of way was only shown as a footpath on a definitive map, the court can still hold that it was a 'road', *Attorney General v Honeywill and Others* [1972] 3 All ER 641.

■ **5(a) 'without due care and attention'**

'Due care and attention' is normally used when the defendant has been careless or has been momentarily inattentive.

It can be proved by witnesses stating that they saw the defendant 'drive round the roundabout and wander into the side of another car' or 'brake rather late and run into the car in front' or by the defendant stating that 'I misjudged the gap or distance' or 'I didn't see the other car, motorbike, cycle or pedestrian, etc'.

■ **5(b) 'without reasonable consideration for other persons using the road'.**

In practice 'without reasonable consideration for other road users' can be proved by a statement from a witness who saw the actions which amount to lack of consideration.

The defendant may wish to make a statement under caution which may prove or help to prove these elements.

(D) SUPPORTING EVIDENCE

Generally the following excuses etc are pertinent to this offence:

(a) Automatism: Any involuntary movement of body or limb, eg epileptic fit, or under attack from a swarm of bees. This is usually a good defence and should be borne in mind when preparing the case.

(b) The offender's non-observance of other vehicles or traffic signs etc is generally no defence, eg 'I didn't see the other car' or 'I didn't see the "stop" sign'.

(c) Excuses based on weather conditions, visibility and the condition of the road surface etc are generally poor defences, unless the driver takes immediate evasive action. Where a driver says 'I was blinded by the sun' or 'There was a patch of fog' or 'The road was covered with black ice', he should have stopped, reduced his speed or driven at a speed which was safe. If he drove on regardless of the conditions he could well be convicted.

When compiling a case, attention must be paid to the prevailing conditions, especially where relevant excuses are put forward, eg in a case where the effect of weather may be a possible defence.

(d) Mechanical defect: The defence of any mechanical defect that caused or contributed towards the offence is normally good. But where the defect or fault should have been detected during normal maintenance, this would not constitute a defence and there would probably be an offence under the appropriate Construction and Use Regulations. In the case of *R v Spurge* [1961] 2 All ER 688 it was held that it was at least careless driving where the driver took a vehicle on a road, knowing there was a defect such as defective steering or brakes.

(e) Defences based on matters outside the driver's control, such as a dog running into the path of the car or a tree being blown across the road are generally good. The presence of the dog at the time of the offence is hard to disprove in the absence of the dead or injured dog, or a witness.

(f) The Highway Code does not create offences but can be quoted by the prosecution or defence to help negate or establish liability.

(g) Evidence of speed at the time of the offence can be established from the length of skid marks, the severity of any impact damage or from witnesses etc.

(h) Other minor points which may be helpful would include: the position of the gear lever after an accident; what the speedometer registers if damaged in an accident; the position of other instruments, such as obligatory light switches or windscreen wiper switches; whether the driver had consumed any alcohol prior to the offence (provided the prejudicial value does not outweigh the evidential value of such evidence) and the mechanical condition of the vehicle.

(i) Sudden illness or losing consciousness would normally avail the driver of a defence unless losing consciousness was as a result of the driver's actions such as a deliberate overdose or taking illegal substances.

Note 1. A notice of intended prosecution is required for this offence if no accident has occurred.

Note 2. The two offences created by section 3, ie 'due care' or 'reasonable consideration' should not be charged as alternatives. One or the other should be chosen based on the evidence available.

2. OBSTRUCTION

Regulation 103 Road Vehicle (Construction and Use) Regulations 1986, and sec 42 Road Traffic Act 1988

(A) POINTS TO PROVE

1. That you 2. being the person in charge 3. of a certain motor vehicle (or trailer) namely a .... 4. did cause (or permit) that motor vehicle (or trailer) 5. to stand on a road called .... 6. so as to cause an unnecessary obstruction thereof.

(B) MEANING OF TERMS

■ **1. 'That you'**

Means the identity of the person in charge.

■ **2. 'being the person in charge'**

Means that such a person generally has the keys for the vehicle, but in the vast majority of cases the person 'in charge' will be the driver who parks the vehicle resulting in the obstruction.

■ **3. 'of a certain motor vehicle (or trailer) namely a ....'**

See Glossary for 'motor vehicle' and 'trailer'.

■ **4. did cause (or permit) that motor vehicle or trailer'**
See Glossary.

■ **5. 'to stand on a road called ....'**
Generally 'to stand' means to allow the motor vehicle (or trailer) to remain stationary and does not necessarily mean unattended (*Hinde v Evans* (1906) 70 JP 548) although this will normally be the case.

■ **6. 'so as to cause an unnecessary obstruction thereof'.**
The judges have taken the word 'unnecessary' to mean 'unreasonable', whether or not use amounting to an obstruction was or was not unreasonable use is a question of fact, depending on all the circumstances, including:

    (i)   the length of time the obstruction continued;
    (ii) the place where it occurred;
    (iii) the purpose for which it was done;
    (iv) whether it caused an actual as opposed to a potential obstruction as quoted in *Evans v Barker* [1971] RTR 453. Commonplace obstructions include restricting the width of the road, blocking footpaths if they form part of the road and obstructing pedestrians and vehicles at 'T' junctions and other types of junctions etc.

Note the Middlesex Crown Court case of *Langham v Crisp* [1975] Crim LR 652 where a motorist parked on one side of the road and an obstruction was caused by the subsequent parking of cars opposite. It was held that when the first vehicle parked it was not done 'so as to cause' an unnecessary obstruction.

(C) USUAL METHODS OF PROVING THESE POINTS
■ **1. 'That you'**
See (C)1 of offence 1.

■ **2. 'being the person in charge'**
This point is usually proved by asking the person suspected of parking or causing the vehicle to be parked in the offending position, 'Are you responsible for this vehicle being left in this position?'

■ **3. 'of a certain motor vehicle (or trailer) namely a ....'**
See (C)3 of offence 1.

■ **4. 'did cause (or permit) that motor vehicle (or trailer)'**
See (C)2 of offence 5, although it is felt that 'permit' in this offence means the continuing obstruction while 'cause' deals with the positioning of the vehicle on the road. (See [1975] Crim LR 653.)

■ **5. 'to stand on a road called ....'**
'To stand' can be proved by the police officer who observed the vehicle stationary on a road. For 'road' see (C)4 of offence 1.

■ **6. 'so as to cause an unnecessary obstruction thereof'.**
This point can best be proved by a police officer who observes some actual unnecessary obstruction of the road causing other road users inconvenience, delay, or complete blockage of the road etc. Such evidence is given by phrases including, 'I saw women with prams obstructed by the offending vehicle parking across a pavement'; 'several motor cars had to negotiate carefully and slowly to pass the offending vehicle' etc. A sketch plan may assist the court where the obstruction is difficult to describe in words.

(D) SUPPORTING EVIDENCE

Note 1. A fixed penalty ticket could be issued for this offence.
Note 2. Also be aware of the offence of leaving a vehicle on a road in a potentially dangerous position contrary to section 22 Road Traffic Act 1988. Examples to show the difference this offence and unnecessary obstruction include leaving a vehicle around a blind bend, or just over a humped-back bridge. A notice of intended prosecution is required for this offence.
Note 3. Also be aware of the offence of wilfully obstructing the free passage of a highway with anything - not just a vehicle - contrary to the Highways Act 1980, section 137. This offence carries a power of arrest for a constable who witnesses the obstruction.

3. FAILING TO STOP AFTER AN ACCIDENT
Section 170 Road Traffic Act 1988

(A) POINTS TO PROVE
1. That you 2. being the driver 3. of a certain mechanically propelled vehicle, namely ....
4. owing to the presence of which 5. on a road called .... 6. an accident occurred whereby injury was caused to another person (or damage was caused to another vehicle or to an animal or to property) 7. did fail to stop.

(B) MEANING OF TERMS
■ 1. 'That you'
Means the person driving the motor vehicle, ie, his identity.
■ 2. 'being the driver'
'Driver' means the person who takes the motor vehicle on the road and he continues to be the driver until the journey is finished, although he may have stopped and switched the engine off some minutes before: *Jones v Prothero* [1952] 1 All ER 434.

A person who has parked his car on a road and left it unattended can't be said to be the driver for the purposes of this offence.
■ 3. 'of a certain mechanically propelled vehicle namely ....'
See (C)3 of offence 1.
■ 4. 'owing to the presence of which'
This point means that there must be a direct connection between the motor vehicle and the occurrence of the accident: *Quelch v Phipps* [1955] 2 All ER 302. Therefore a passenger jumping off a moving bus and injuring himself would bring the motor vehicle within this section, but not generally where a driver has left his stationary motor vehicle parked on a road.
■ 5. 'on a road called ....'
See (C)3 of offence 1.

■ 6. 'an accident occurred whereby injury was caused to another person (or damage was caused to another vehicle or to an animal or to property)'

'Accident' means an unintended occurrence which has an adverse physical result (*R v Morris* [1972] 1 All ER 384). It can also include an accident resulting from a deliberate act (*Chief Constable of West Midlands Police v Billingham* [1979] Crim LR 256). No other vehicle need be involved as where a person or animal or property is involved (*R v Pico* [1971] Crim LR 599).

'Injury' includes shock, or a hysterical and nervous condition (*R v Miller* [1954] 2 All ER 529 and *Bourhill v Young* [1943] AC 92.

'Another person' means other than the driver, therefore where only the driver is injured this section is not applicable.

'To another vehicle' means that damage must be caused to a vehicle other than the driver's motor vehicle. Therefore where only the driver's motor vehicle is damaged the section does not apply. Note that this phrase applies to 'another vehicle' and not 'another motor vehicle'. 'Vehicle' has been held to include a bicycle (*Ellis v Nott-Bower* [1896] 60 JP 760).

'Animal' means horse, cattle, ass, mule, sheep, pig goat or dog. Notable exceptions are cats and poultry.

'Property' means property growing in, constructed on, fixed to, or forming part of, the land adjacent to the road or on the road itself. Therefore trees, crops, lampposts, traffic signs, walls etc will generally be included in section 170.

■ 7. 'did fail to stop'.

Means did fail to stop immediately the accident happened and remain at the scene of the accident long enough, taking the prevailing conditions into account, to give his name and address and also the name and address of the owner and the identification marks of the vehicle (*Lee v Knapp* [1966] 3 All ER 961 and *Ward v Rawson* [1979] Crim LR 58). The obligation to stop arises almost immediately the accident happens. The driver should stop almost immediately, as soon as it is convenient and safe to do so (*Hallinan v DPP* [1998] Crim LR754). Two separate offences are created by section 170, namely (1) failing to stop and (2) failing to give particulars (*Roper v Sullivan* [1978] Crim LR 233).

If a motor vehicle is stationary when the accident occurs the driver must remain at the scene until he has satisfied the section. But note that he need not wait indefinitely (*Norling v Woolacott* [1964] SASR 377).

(C) USUAL METHODS OF PROVING THESE POINTS
■ 1. 'That you'
See (C)1 of offence 1.
■ 2. 'being the driver'
This point will be proved by a witness seeing the defendant driving away etc. Where there are no witnesses or they cannot be traced, an admission by the defendant either verbally to the officer dealing with the case (who would record the admission in his pocket book or accident booklet) or in writing if he chooses to make a 'voluntary' statement in accordance with the Codes of Practice.

Also see (C)2 of offence 1.
■ 3. 'of certain mechanically propelled vehicle, namely ....'
See (C)3 of offence 1.
■ 4. 'owing to the presence of which'
This point is normally covered in any witness statement that might be available, viz, 'I saw four vehicles were involved etc' or 'if it had not been for that vehicle the accident would not have happened'. Where witnesses are unavailable an admission to being involved is helpful.
■ 5. 'on a road called ....'
See (C)4 of offence 1.

■ 6. 'an accident occurred whereby injury was caused to another person (or damage was caused to another vehicle or to an animal or to property)'

This point is normally proved by the police officer examining the vehicles concerned or person, animal or property involved and recording the details of damage or injury in his pocket book or accident booklet. Where a person is injured it is normal practice to take a statement to the effect that 'the following injuries were sustained'. In some cases of damage it might be wise to ascertain whether or not there was any similar damage prior to the accident. In this way a defence that the property was already damaged and that the defendant is not responsible for the present damage can be countered.

■ 7. 'did fail to stop'.

It is rare for a police officer to witness such an event, therefore in most cases the evidence of passers-by or the driver of the other vehicle involved will have to be relied upon.

Obviously, the best kind of evidence in such cases is the evidence of 'independent' witnesses, ie a witness not concerned with the parties involved in the accident. Where the only evidence available is that of one party against the other, or a wife giving evidence for her husband, or an employee giving evidence for the employer etc the court may well find the case not proved.

A good practical point to include is a statement that there was an interested party at the scene, had the defendant stopped. In other words, an injured pedestrian or the driver of a damaged vehicle had remained at the scene. Had the defendant stopped he could have given his particulars to such a person.

(D) SUPPORTING EVIDENCE

This offence was absolute, ie no *mens rea* was required. However in *Harding v Price* [1948] 1 All ER 283 it was held that if the driver did not know he had been involved in an accident the section did not apply. Therefore in borderline cases the prosecution might have to rely on evidence of the severity of injury and damage, or the noise of the accident, to help prove to the court beyond all reasonable doubt that the driver must have realised that he had been involved in an accident.

An example of when a driver may not be aware of an accident would be if a large articulated motor vehicle, when turning a sharp corner, had a slight collision with a parked car. If the police could not prove that the accident was of such force and severity that the driver must have known of the accident, then the defence could put forward the saving in *Harding v Price*.

Note. As section 170 creates two offences, if the defendant fails to stop but later reports the accident, or stops but refuses to give any particulars, an offence is committed as per *North v Gerish* (1959) 123 JP 313.

4. DISQUALIFIED DRIVING
Section 103(1)(b) Road Traffic Act 1988

(A) POINTS TO PROVE
1. That you 2. being disqualified for holding or obtaining a licence to drive a motor vehicle (if of a certain class, state) 3. drove a certain motor vehicle, namely a .... (if of a certain class, state) 4. on a road called ....

(B) MEANING OF TERMS
■ 1. 'That you'
Means the person driving the motor vehicle, ie identify the driver.
■ 2. 'being disqualified for holding or obtaining a licence to drive a motor vehicle'
Disqualification means that the person disqualified must not, in Great Britain, drive on a road any motor vehicle.

■ **3. 'did drive a certain motor vehicle, namely a ....'**
See (C)2 of offence 1.
■ **4. 'on a road called ....'.**
See (C)4 of offence 1.

(C) USUAL METHODS OF PROVING THESE POINTS
■ **1. 'That you'**
See (C)1 of offence 1; also *R v Turnbull and Others* in Glossary, 'That you'.
■ **2. 'being disqualified for holding or obtaining a licence to drive a motor vehicle'**
Proof of disqualification may be certificate of conviction or extract from the magistrates' court's register together with proof of identification of the defendant, eg by the police officer who was present in court when the defendant was disqualified. This procedure varies according to local practice and inquiries regarding the best method of proof are advised.
■ **3. did drive a certain motor vehicle, namely a ....'**
See (C)2 and 3 of offence 1.
■ **4. 'on a road called ....'.** See (C)4 of offence 1.

(D) SUPPORTING EVIDENCE
Problems related to the identity of the driver occur quite frequently with this offence. A police officer may see a person driving a motor vehicle, whom he knows to be disqualified, but is not in a position to stop the driver. When eventually interviewed regarding the suspected offence there may be a denial and, while not essential, the prosecution case would be stronger if corroboration is available regarding the driver's identity. (See the eight points of *R v Turnbull and Others* in Glossary, 'That you'.)

Note 1. Where a defendant states that he did not know that he was disqualified this will not amount to a defence, *Taylor v Kenyon* [1952] 2 All ER 726.

Note 2. An under-age driver should be prosecuted for not having the appropriate driving licence, not for the above offence.

Note 3. There is a power of arrest on reasonable suspicion of this offence but only when seen driving, although the **general arrest** conditions could apply.

5. USING ETC WITHOUT INSURANCE
Section 143 Road Traffic Act 1988

(A) POINTS TO PROVE
1. That you 2. did use (or cause, or permit .... to use) 3. a motor vehicle, namely a .... 4. on a road called .... 5. there not being in force in relation to the use of that vehicle 6. such a policy of insurance or security 7. in respect of third party risks as complies with the requirements of Part VI, Road Traffic Act 1988.

(B) MEANING OF TERMS
■ 1. 'That you'

Means the person using, causing or permitting the use of the motor vehicle ie identify the offender.

■ 2. 'did use (or cause, or permit .... to use)'

See Glossary.

■ 3. 'a motor vehicle, namely a ....'

See Glossary.

■ 4. 'on a road called ....'

See (C) 4 of offence 1.

■ 5. 'there not being in force in relation to the use of that vehicle'

This phrase means that there is no insurance cover in force relating to the use of the vehicle as opposed to insurance covering the contents for example.

■ 6. 'such a policy of insurance or security'

A policy is of no effect until the certificate is delivered to the assured (section 147(1) Road Traffic Act 1988). The policy is the contractual document setting out the terms and conditions of the insurance agreement which appear in various paragraphs which are usually called clauses.

■ **7. 'in respect of third party risks as complies with the requirements of Part VI Road Traffic Act 1988'.**

Section 145 Road Traffic Act 1988 sets out the requirements for third part risks as follows.

'(2) The policy must be issued by an authorised insurer.

'(3) Subject to subsection (4) below, the policy:

(a) must insure such person, persons or classes of persons as may be specified in the policy in respect of any liability which may be incurred by him or them in respect of the death of or bodily injury to any person caused by, or arising out of, the use of the vehicle on a road in Great Britain; and,

(aa) must, in the case of a vehicle normally based in the territory of another member state, insure him or them in respect of any civil liability which may be incurred by him or them as a result of an event related to the use of the vehicle in Great Britain...

(b) must in the case of a vehicle normally based in Great Britain, insure him or them in respect of any liability which may be incurred by him or them in respect of the use of the vehicle and of any trailer, whether or not coupled, in the territory other than Great Britain and Gibraltar of each of the member states of the Communities according to... the law on compulsory insurance against civil liability in respect of the use of vehicles of the state where the liability may be incurred; ...and

(c) must also insure him or them in respect of any liability which may be incurred by him or them under the provisions of this Part of this Act relating to payment for emergency treatment.

'(4) The policy shall not by virtue of subsection (3)(a) above, be required to cover:

(a) liability in respect of the death, arising out of and in the course of his employment, of a person in the employment of a person insured by the policy or of bodily injury sustained by such a person arising out of and in the course of his employment; or, [other such matters. (See section for full list.)]'

(C) USUAL METHODS OF PROVING THESE POINTS

■ 1. 'That you'
See (C)1 of offence 1.

■ 2. 'did use (or cause, or permit .... to use)'
'Use' is generally proved by the observation of the police officer to the effect, 'I stopped the motor vehicle .... which was being driven in Queens Street and spoke to the driver ....'

A few offences of this nature will involve the owner of the vehicle or employer of the driver. For example the owner of a motor vehicle can be said to use it where he sits at the side of the driver, who is not his employee and the vehicle is being used for his purpose (*Cobb v Williams* [1973] RTR 113).

An employer uses the vehicle even when he is not present in it, when it is being used on his business, with his permission. Therefore, where the driver is accompanied by the owner, or the motor vehicle is being used on firm's business, the driver and the owner or employer all 'use'.

Where the owner is present in the vehicle the police officer's statement will include an admission as to the vehicle's ownership eg, 'Are you the owner of this vehicle?' and the passenger replies, 'Yes'.

In cases involving an employer he will probably have to be interviewed later. Questions such as, 'Are you the company secretary or owner of .... firm?'; 'Is your firm the owner of motor vehicle ....?' and 'Was it being used on firm's business at ..... (time) ..... in ..... (place) ..... ?', need affirmative answers.

He can then be cautioned and reported for the 'using' offence. Note that a person does not use a vehicle without insurance unless there is an element of controlling, managing and operating the vehicle.

'Cause' can be proved by questions and answers or by instructions written on a job-sheet etc.

Knowledge of the facts amounting to the unlawful use must be shown in the statement of evidence. The driver may provide information that his boss said words to the effect that he knew there was no insurance but the vehicle was the only one available and the journey had to be undertaken.

It has been held that towing a vehicle is 'causing' it to be used (*Milstead v Sexton* [1964] Crim LR 474).

'Permit' is not as precise a term as 'cause' and denotes an express or inferred permission of a general or particular type. Again the prosecution must rely on what the driver tells them or on written instructions and, in rare cases, on admissions by the employer.

'Use' is to be preferred as a charge on the grounds that it is easier to prove, being a clearly defined term, and attracts fewer defences than 'cause' and 'permits'.

■ **3. 'a motor vehicle, namely a ....'**

See (C)3 of offence 1.

■ **4. 'on a road called ....'**

See (C)4 of offence 1.

■ **5. 'there not being in force in relation to the use of that vehicle'**

The proof of insurance falls to the defence once it has been established by the prosecution that the motor vehicle has been used on a road (*Philcox v Carberry* [1960] Crim LR 563).

While the onus is on the defence, most police officers' statements contain the question: 'Are you insured to drive this motor vehicle?' In the cases where an expired insurance certificate is produced a question such as, 'have you any other insurance for this motor vehicle?' is advisable.

■ 6. 'such a policy of insurance or security'

The prosecution must show that the insurance, if any is produced, does not conform to the requirements of section 143 Road Traffic Act 1988, as section 147(1) of that Act requires that for a policy to be effective, the insurers must deliver a certificate in the prescribed form to the assured. The courts recognise the insurance certificate as evidence of being insured. Therefore the police generally require to see the certificate to satisfy themselves that the motor vehicle is correctly insured but in some cases of doubt the policy may have to be examined or inquiries made of the issuing firm.

Evidence of insufficient cover might include someone other than the insured person driving the vehicle; the vehicle being used for the purpose other than agreed, eg for business purposes; or the present vehicle not being entered on the firm's records (this being difficult to detect in these days of not generally showing a registered number on a certificate).

■ 7. 'in respect of third party risks as complies with the requirements of Part VI, Road Traffic Act 1988'.

The police officer will normally accept the information on the insurance certificate at face value and if the certificate shows 'comprehensive' cover, this automatically includes 'third party risks'. In a large number of cases the cover will be restricted to 'third party' only which is still within the requirements of section 145 above, at point (B)7 of this offence.

(D) SUPPORTING EVIDENCE

Note 1. When a certificate of insurance has expired or when a new insurance contract is being negotiated, insurance companies issue 'cover notes' which usually vary in length of validity from 15 days to 60 days.

Note 2. For a cover note to be valid the defendant must accept the cover note and rely upon it for his insurance cover. If he disregards it because he intends to insure with another firm, for example, and never pays the original firm, the cover note will not be valid *(Taylor v Allon [1965] 1 All ER 557)*.

Note 3. As with numerous other offences dealing with road traffic, the use of a motor vehicle without insurance is an absolute offence, ie no guilty knowledge is required.

Note 4. Occasionally when an employee is found to be driving whilst uninsured on his employer's business he can put forward a defence where he shows:

    (a)   the vehicle did not belong to him; and

    (b)   was not in his possession under a contract of hire or loan; and

    (c)   that he neither knew nor had reason to believe he was driving without insurance.

The employer could still commit the offence of using, causing or permitting no insurance.

6. USING ETC WITHOUT A TEST CERTIFICATE
Section 47 (1) Road Traffic Act 1988

(A) POINTS TO PROVE
    1. That you 2. did use (or cause, or permit to be used)
    3. on a road called .... 4. a motor vehicle, namely
    a .... (specify type of motor vehicle) to which section
    47 of the Road Traffic Act 1988, applied and
    5. in respect of which no test certificate had been issued
    within 12 months prior to the .... day of .... year
    ....

(B) MEANING OF TERMS
■ 1. 'That you'
Means the person using or permitting the use of the motor vehicle, ie identify the driver etc.

■ **2. 'did use (or cause, or permit to be used)'**
See Glossary.

■ **3. 'on a road called ....'**
See Glossary.

■ **4. 'a motor vehicle, namely a .... to which section 47 of the Road Traffic Act 1988 applied and'**
See Glossary.

Section 47 applies to all motor vehicles first used more than three years before the time at which they are proved to have been actually used on the road for the purpose of the present offence.

The Motor Vehicles (Tests) Regulations 1981 exempt, among other motor vehicles, goods vehicles of an unladen weight exceeding 3,500kg; an agricultural motor vehicle; articulated vehicles; when submitting a vehicle for a test after prior arrangement or bringing it away; where a test certificate is refused - taking it for repair by prior arrangement or bringing it away and also taking it, by towing, to be broken up and motor traders when repairing motor vehicles etc.

■ **5. 'in respect of which no test certificate had been issued within 12 months prior to the .... day of ....'.**
This phrase means there was no current test certificate in force for the motor vehicle. A test certificate is valid for 12 months.

(C) USUAL METHODS OF PROVING THESE POINTS

■ **1. 'That you'**
See (C)1 of offence 1.

■ **2. 'did use (or cause, or permit to be used)'**
See Glossary.

■ **3. 'on a road called ....**
See Glossary.

■ **4. 'a motor vehicle, namely a .... to which section 47 of the Road Traffic Act 1988, applied and'**
See Glossary for 'motor vehicle'. Proof that the motor vehicle required a test certificate is often overlooked. The majority of

this kind of offence will be concerned with motor cars, but whenever the vehicle is of an unusual type the exemptions to the requirements must be carefully checked. Once it has been established that the vehicle or its use is not exempt from the requirement, the type of motor vehicle should be described in the statement. The second requirement is that the date of first registration is more than three years from the date of the suspected offence. Normally this point is proved by the officer in the case examining the registration document and including in his statement a passage such as, 'On examining the vehicle's registration document I saw the date of first registration was ....'. If the registration document is lost, or at the DVLA, Swansea, then proof can be requested from the DVLA.

■ **5. 'in respect of which no test certificate had been issued within 12 months prior to the .... day of ....'.**
As with other documents which can be obtained at a large number of different places, the onus to show that the vehicle had a current test certificate rests on the defendant. An expired certificate might be produced. The particulars should be entered in the police officer's pocket book and followed by a question such as, 'Have you any other test certificate for this motor vehicle?' The driver might admit he hasn't a current certificate and the relevant conversation can be reproduced in the officer's statement of evidence.

(D) SUPPORTING EVIDENCE

If a police officer has to request a driver to produce a current test certificate, the officer must bear in mind the problem of proving the date of first registration. If a form HO/RT 1 is issued and the driver elects to produce the document at a distant police station it is good practice also to request the suspected driver to produce his registration document at the same time. In this way the officer accepting the production can also prove the date of first registration, if need be by personal appearance.

7. NO CRASH HELMET

Regulation 4 Motor Cycles (Protective Helmets)
Regulations 1998 and section 16 Road Traffic Act
1988

(A) POINTS TO PROVE

1. That you 2. did drive (or ride on) 3. a certain motor
bicycle, namely a .... 4. on a road called ....
5. without protective headgear.

(B) MEANING OF TERMS

■ 1. 'That you'

Means the person driving or riding on the motor bicycle, ie the
identity.

■ 2. 'did drive (or ride on)'

'Or ride on' includes any pillion passenger, but not passengers
in any sidecar, per regulation 3(1) of the above Regulations.

■ 3. 'a certain motor bicycle, namely a ....'

Means a two wheeled motor cycle, whether having a sidecar
attached thereto or not, and for the purposes of this definition
any wheels of a motor cycle shall, if the distance between the
centres of the areas of contact between such wheels and the road
surface is less than 460 millimetres, be counted as one wheel;
per regulation 4(3) of the Regulations. A mowing machine
coming within the definition of a motor bicycle is exempt. The
offence does not include propelling the motor bicycle by a person on foot.

■ 4. 'on a road called ....'

See Glossary.

■ 5. 'without protective headgear'.

'Without' could mean either no headgear at all or a headgear
which is not 'protective headgear' as defined: 'protective headgear' means headgear which:

(a) is either -

(i) a helmet bearing a marking applied by the manufacturer indicating compliance with the specification contained in one of the British Standards mentioned in Schedule 2 (whether or not as modified by any amendment), or

(ii) a helmet of a type manufactured for use by persons on motor cycles which by virtue of its shape, material and construction could reasonably be expected to afford to persons on motor bicycles a degree of protection from injury in the event of an accident similar to or greater than that provided by the helmet of a type complying with one of the specifications referred to in the preceding sub-paragraph; and

(b) if worn with a chin cup attached to or held in position by a strap or other fastening provided on the helmet, is provided with an additional strap or other fastening (to be fastened under the wearer's jaw) for securing the helmet firmly to the head of the wearer; and

(c) is securely fastened to the head of the wearer by means of the straps or other fastening provided on the headgear for that purpose.

(C) USUAL METHODS OF PROVING THESE POINTS

■ 1. 'That you'
Can be proved as (C)1 of offence 1.

■ 2. 'did drive (or ride on)'
See (C)2 of offence 1 for 'drive'. 'Ride on' can be proved by the police officer or witness who saw the offence.

■ 3. 'a certain motor bicycle, namely a ....'
In the vast majority of cases the offender(s) will be on a solo motor bicycle, and occasionally one having a sidecar attached. This fact can be mentioned in the police officer's statement of evidence if he witnessed the offence.

■ 4. 'on a road called ....'
See Glossary; also (C)4 of offence 1.

■ **5. 'without protective headgear'.**

This point can be proved by the police officer's observations that the person on the motor bicycle had no headgear or the headgear he was wearing did not come within the legal requirements. Where it is suspected that headgear is below the British Standard the assistance of a Forensic Science Laboratory could be sought. If the securing straps are not within the legal requirements a full description will be necessary.

(D) SUPPORTING EVIDENCE

Note. The Regulations provide the following exemption. 'A requirement imposed by regulations shall not apply to any follower of the Sikh religion while he is wearing a turban.'

8. NO VEHICLE LICENCE
Section 29(1) and (3) Vehicle Excise and Registration Act 1994 and section 44 of the Magistrates' Courts Act 1980

(A) POINTS TO PROVE
1. That you 2. did use (or keep) 3. a mechanically propelled vehicle, namely a .... 4. on a public road called .... 5. for which a vehicle licence was not in force.

(B) MEANING OF TERMS
■ **1. 'That you'**
Means the person using/keeping the motor vehicle, ie their identity.
■ **2. 'did use (or keep)'**
A person 'keeps' a vehicle if he causes it to be stationary on a road when not in use. The shortness of the period of time it is left on the road is immaterial (*Holliday v Henry* [1974] RTR 101).

■ **3. 'a mechanically propelled vehicle, namely a ....'**
Means propelled by petrol, oil, steam or electricity etc. A vehicle ceases to be mechanically propelled when there is no reasonable prospect of it ever being mobile again (*Binks v Department of the Environment* [1975] RTR 318). Certain vehicles are exempt from duty under various Acts. Exemptions likely to be encountered include vehicles not exceeding 10cwt unladen specially adapted for invalids; vehicles brought from abroad for a temporary stay are exempt for a period not exceeding one year from date of importation; vehicles going to or returning from a vehicle test or being repaired etc as a result of the test, provided in all cases prior arrangements have been made. Lists of exemptions can be found in Schedule 2 of the Act.

■ **4. 'on a public road called ....'**
'Public road' means 'a road which is repairable at the public expense', per section 62.

■ **5. 'for which a vehicle licence was not in force'.**
This phrase means that there was no current vehicle licence in force and this point can be verified by making inquiries at the DVLA, Swansea. A licence is void from the time it was granted where the payment was by a cheque which was eventually dishonoured (Customs and Excise Management Act).

(C) USUAL METHODS OF PROVING THESE POINTS
■ **1. 'That you'**
See (C)1 of offence 1.

■ **2. 'did use (or keep)'**
'Use' is usually proved by the police officer in the case giving evidence that he saw the defendant driving the motor vehicle in question. Traffic wardens can also become involved with this offence by detecting a vehicle not displaying a current vehicle licence. Where subsequent inquiries show the vehicle to be unlicensed, the traffic warden would be able to prove use. Similarly, where a vehicle is seen stationary and unattended, the offence of

'keeping' can be considered. The officer who saw the vehicle being kept should be in a position to state the length of time he observed the vehicle being kept on a public road, but see point (B)2 of this offence regarding the length of time kept being immaterial.

Proof of ownership is not required to establish who 'used' or 'kept' the vehicle, but it is advisable that the prosecution should know the owner of the vehicle. An employer is liable for the offence of 'using' an unlicensed vehicle if the vehicle is driven on his business and it is no defence for the employer to show that he had not authorised the journey if, in fact, the journey was on his business (*Richardson v Baker* [1976] RTR 56). The burden of proof regarding the purpose for which the vehicle was used lies on the defence, section 53.

■ 3. 'a mechanically propelled vehicle, namely a ....'
This point is proved by describing the vehicle concerned and making sure it does not come with the many exemptions. 'Mechanically propelled vehicle' does not mean the same as 'motor vehicle' as defined in the Glossary. For the purposes of the Vehicles Excise and Registration Act the vehicle need not be intended or adapted for use on a road. In cases of difficulty the test as mentioned at (B)3 of this offence, ie will the vehicle ever be mobile again, might help in cases where parts have been taken off a vehicle.

■ 4. 'on a public road called ....'
No offence against section 29 is committed where the vehicle is used or kept on a private road, ie a road which is not repairable at public expense. The highways department of the local authority will be able to prove which roads are repairable at public expense where necessary.

■ 5. 'for which a vehicle licence was not in force'.
This point can be proved by an admission on the part of the defendant; on inquiries at the DVLA, Swansea whose records can be produced in evidence; and by an admission on the part of the owner where he isn't the defendant etc.

(D) SUPPORTING EVIDENCE

Note. It has been said in the case of *Carpenter v Campbell* [1953] 1 All ER 280 that it may be an oppressive course to prosecute the driver of an unlicensed vehicle in a master-servant relationship, where the driver is the employee and not responsible for licensing the vehicle.

9. MISUSE OF A TRADE LICENCE (OR TRADE PLATES)

Regulations 35 Road Vehicles (Registration and Licensing) Regulations 1971 and sections 11, 12 and 34 Vehicle Excise and Registration Act 1994

(A) POINTS TO PROVE

1. **That you being the holder of a trade licence (or licences) issued under section 11 Vehicle Excise and Registration Act 1994 2. used by virtue of that (or those) licence (or licences) 3. on a public road called .... 4. a vehicle, namely a .... 5. for a purpose other than a purpose prescribed under section 12 Vehicle Excise and Registration Act 1994 .... (specify purpose).**

(B) MEANING OF TERMS

■ 1. **'That you being the holder of a trade licence issued under section 11 Vehicle Excise and Registration Act 1994'**
This means that the defendant must be the person to whom the trade licence was issued. In a large number of cases the licence is issued to a firm, ie a limited company, then the company secretary is liable for the misuse of the trade plate on behalf of the company. The holder of the licence must be a motor trader, vehicle tester or vehicle manufacturer. His identity must be proved.

■ 2. 'used by virtue of that licence'

In other words the vehicle concerned must have been used under the trade licence and not under a normal vehicle excise licence for an offence to contravene the law relating to trade licences.

■ 3. 'on a public road called ....'

See (B)4 of offence 8.

■ 4. 'a vehicle, namely a ....'

See (B)3 of offence 8 for vehicles concerned.

■ 5. 'for the purpose other than a purpose prescribed under section 12 Vehicle Excise and Registration Act 1994'

Namely in the Road Vehicles (Registration and Licensing) Regulations 1971, regulation 35:

(1) In this regulation, 'business purpose', in relation to a motor trader means:

    (a) a purpose connected with his business as a manufacturer or repairer of or dealer in mechanically propelled vehicles; or

    (b) a purpose connected with his business as a manufacturer or repairer of or dealer in trailers carried on in conjunction with his business as a motor trader, and

    (c) a purpose connected with his business of modifying vehicles prior to the first registration... or of valeting vehicles.

(2) For the purposes of sub-paragraphs (a) to (k) of paragraph (4) of this regulation, where a mechanically propelled vehicle is used on a public road by virtue of a trade licence and that vehicle is drawing a trailer, the vehicle and trailer shall be deemed to constitute a single vehicle.

(3) Save as provided in regulation 36 of these regulations, no person, being a motor trader and the holder of a trade vehicle, shall use any mechanically propelled vehicle on a public road by virtue of that licence unless it is a vehicle which is temporarily in his possession in the course of his business as

a motor trader or a recovery vehicle kept by him for the purpose of dealing with disabled vehicles in the course of that business.

(4) Save as provided in the said regulation 36 and without derogation from the provisions of the last preceding paragraph of this regulation, no person, being a motor trader and the holder of a trade licence, shall use any mechanically propelled vehicle on a public road by virtue of that licence for a purpose other than a business purpose and other than one of the following purposes:

(a) for its test or trial or the test or trial of its accessories or equipment in the ordinary course of construction, modification or repair or after completion in either such case;

(b) for proceeding to or from a public weighbridge for ascertaining its unladen weight or to or from any place for its registration or inspection by a person acting on behalf of the Secretary of State;

(c) for its test or trial for the benefit of a prospective purchaser, for proceeding at the instance of a prospective purchaser to any place for the purpose of such test or trial, or for returning after such test or trial;

(d) for its test or trial for the benefit of a person interested in promoting publicity in regard to it, for proceeding at the instance of such a person to any place for the purpose of such test or trial, or for returning after such test or trial;

(e) for delivering it to the place where the purchaser intends to keep it;

(f) for demonstrating its operation or the operation of its accessories or equipment when being handed over to the purchaser;

(g) for delivering it from one part of his premises to another part of his premises, or for delivering it from his premises to the premises of, or between parts of premises of, another manufacturer or repairer of or dealer in mechanically propelled vehicles or removing it from the premises of another manufacturer or repairer of or dealer in mechanically propelled vehicles direct to his own premises;

(h) for proceeding to or returning from a workshop in which a body or a special type of equipment or accessory is to be or has been fitted to it or in which it is to be or has been painted, valeted or repaired;

(i) for proceeding from the premises of a manufacturer or repairer of or dealer in mechanically propelled vehicles to a place from which it is to be transported by train, ship or aircraft or for proceeding to the premises of such a manufacturer, repairer or dealer from a place to which it has been so transported;

(j) for proceeding to or returning from any garage, auction room or other place at which vehicles are usually stored or usually or periodically offered for sale and at which the vehicle is to be or has been stored or is to be or has been offered for sale as the case may be;

(k) for proceeding to or returning from a place where it is to be or has been tested, or for proceeding to a place where it is to be broken up or otherwise dismantled.

(C) USUAL METHODS OF PROVING THESE POINTS

■ 1. 'that you being the holder of a trade licence issued under section 11 Vehicle Excise and Registration Act 1994'

Has a slightly different meaning than the offence where the driver is required to be identified. In this case the prosecution must prove that the person who has been summonsed is the holder of the trade licence. In some cases he will be the driver of the vehicle. It can be proved that he was the holder by examining the trade licence itself for the defendant's name, by an admission from the defendant and by checking with the issuing authority.

■ 2. 'used by virtue of that licence'

This point can be proved by asking the trade licence holder 'was (or is) this vehicle being used under this trade licence?' If the vehicle is driven by an employee who is not to be summonsed for any offence, a statement should be requested as he should be dealt with as a witness. He should be asked to mention in his statement the fact that the vehicle was being used by virtue of the trade licence.

■ 3. 'on a public road called ....'

See the comments made at offence 8(C)4, ie the road must be repairable at public expense.

■ 4. 'a vehicle, namely a ....'

As excise duty is the subject matter of this offence the same vehicles that are exempt from vehicle excise licences are also exempt from the necessity for a trade licence, therefore refer to offence 8(C)3 for more information.

■ 5. 'for a purpose other than a purpose prescribed under section 12 Vehicle Excise and Registration Act 1994'.

The purpose is proved by question and answer if the defendant is driving or if he has to be interviewed later by a police officer. A statement from any employee who could help prove this point would be valuable for the prosecution, especially if it is suspected the defence will deny the alleged purpose. The garage foreman who perhaps sent the employee driver on the journey could be asked to provide a statement. Illegal uses often include shopping trips, collecting spare parts for the garage or calling at a public house along a journey. Each use will present its own problems of proof and it is impossible to lay down any hard and fast rules.

(D) SUPPORTING EVIDENCE

Where the prosecution allege a contravention of the trade plate law there will probably be the further offence of 'no vehicle licence', see offence 8.

10. WINDSCREEN WASHERS NOT FITTED OR NOT WORKING

Regulation 34(2) Road Vehicles (Construction and Use) Regulations 1986 and section 42 Road Traffic Act 1988

(A) POINTS TO PROVE

1. That you 2. did use (or cause, or permit to be used) 3. on the road called .... 4. a motor vehicle namely a .... 5. which was required to be fitted with windscreen wipers 6. which was not fitted with windscreen washers capable of cleaning in conjunction with those wipers the area of windscreen swept by the wipers.

(B) MEANING OF TERMS

■ 1. 'That you'

Means the user's etc identity.

■ 2. 'did use (or cause, or permit to be used)'

See Glossary.

■ 3. 'on a road called ....'

See Glossary.

■ 4. 'a motor vehicle namely a ....'

See Glossary.

■ 5. 'which was required to be fitted with windscreen wipers'

This point means that regulation 34(1) of the above regulations requires every vehicle which is fitted with a windscreen to be fitted with one or more wipers.

One exception to this requirement is in circumstances in which a view to the front can be obtained without first looking through the windscreen, for example, by opening or looking over it.

■ **6. 'which was not fitted with windscreen washers capable of cleaning in conjunction with those wipers the area of windscreen swept by the wipers'.**

This point means that where a motor vehicle is required to be fitted with wipers it must also have washers. The washers must be correctly aligned, filled with fluid and be otherwise correctly maintained, so as to be capable of cleaning in conjunction with the wipers.

(C) USUAL METHODS OF PROVING THESE POINTS
■ **1. 'That you'**
See (C)1 of offence 1.
■ **2. 'did use (or cause, or permit to be used)'**
See (C)2 of offences 5 and 19.
■ **3. 'on a road called ....'**
See (C)4 of offence 1.
■ **4. 'a motor vehicle namely a ....'**
See (C)3 of offence 1.
■ **5. 'which was required to be fitted with windscreen wipers'**

This point is proved by showing there was no view to the front without first looking through the windscreen. This point is usually included in the police officer's statement of evidence, eg, 'The driver could not get a view to the front without first looking through the windscreen'.

■ **6. 'which was not fitted with windscreen washers capable of cleaning in conjunction with those wipers the area of windscreen swept by the wipers'.**

This point can be proved by showing in the police officer's evidence the actual situation regarding washers, ie whether any washers were fitted; if fitted, whether there was any fluid in the reservoir; or whether the jets were correctly adjusted etc. The main point to show is that the washers were not capable of cleaning as required.

11. LIGHTS IN POOR VISIBILITY CONDITIONS

Regulation 24 Road Vehicles Lighting Regulations
1989 and section 42(1) Road Traffic Act 1988

(A) POINTS TO PROVE

1. That you 2. did use 3. a vehicle namely a ....
4. which carried obligatory lamps 5. on a road called ......
6. between the hours of sunrise and sunset without the
lamps being lit while the vehicle was in motion 7. during
a period of seriously reduced visibility on that road.

(B) MEANING OF TERMS

■ **1. 'That you'**
Means the identity of the person using the vehicle.

■ **2. 'did use'**
See Glossary.

■ **3. 'a vehicle namely a ....'**
The term is wider than motor vehicle and has been held to
include a bicycle

■ **4. 'which carries obligatory lamps'**
'Obligatory lamps', in relation to a vehicle, means such of the
obligatory front lamps, obligatory headlamps and obligatory rear
lamps as the vehicle is required, by virtue of the Road Vehicles
Lighting Regulations, to carry when on a road during the hours of
darkness (as defined by the Road Vehicles Lighting Regulations).

■ **5. 'on a road called'**
See Glossary.

■ **6. 'between the hours of sunrise and sunset without the
lamps being lit while the vehicle was in motion'**
'Without the lamps being lit' is self-explanatory. It is thought
that this means all must be working to comply with this regulation. 'While the vehicle was in motion' means that the vehicle
must be moving either backwards or forwards and that these
regulations do not apply when the vehicle is stationary.

■ 7. 'during a period of seriously reduced visibility conditions on that road'.

'Seriously reduced visibility conditions' in relation to a vehicle used on a road between the hours of sunrise and sunset (ie daytime) may include such conditions adversely affecting visibility (whether consisting of, or including, fog, smoke, heavy rain or spray, snow, dense cloud, or any similar condition) as seriously reduce the ability of the driver (after the appropriate use by him of any windscreen wiper and washer) to see other vehicles or persons on the road, or the ability of other users of the road to see the vehicle.

(C) USUAL METHODS OF PROVING THESE POINTS

■ 1. 'That you'
See (C)1 of offence 1.

■ 2. 'did use'
See (C)2 of offence 5.

3. 'a vehicle namely a ....'
'Vehicle' is proved by describing it in a prosecution witness' statement.

■ 4. 'which carried obligatory lamps'
Can be proved by describing which obligatory lamps it carried in a witness' statement.

■ 5. 'on a road called ....'
See (C)4 of offence 1.

■ 6. 'between the hours of sunrise and sunset without the lamps being lit while the vehicle was in motion'
'The hours of sunrise and sunset' can be proved by reference to an almanac or from a witness' observations if this is found necessary. The lamps not being lit and the motion of the vehicle can be proved by the observations of a prosecution witness, ie usually the constable who reports the offender for summons, eg, 'The vehicle's obligatory lights were not lit and the vehicle was in motion on the road'.

■ **7. 'during a period of seriously reduced visibility conditions on that road'.**

Can be proved by describing the conditions according to the definition at (B)7 of this offence. This is a question of fact for the court to decide and therefore it is essential for the prosecution to show that the conditions seriously reduced the ability of the driver to see other vehicles etc. The offending driver may occasionally admit this fact but failing that the poor visibility must be proved.

(D) SUPPORTING EVIDENCE

Note. Where a headlamp is capable of emitting a dipped beam and a full or main beam, then either beam would be sufficient. A matched pair of front fog lamps can be substituted for headlamps in conditions of fog or falling snow.

12. FAIL TO COMPLY WITH CONSTABLE'S OR WARDEN'S SIGNAL
Section 35(1) Road Traffic Act 1988

(A) POINTS TO PROVE
1. That you 2. being the person driving (or propelling)
3. a vehicle, namely a .... 4. where a police constable (or a traffic warden) was for the time being engaged in the regulation of traffic 5. on a road called ....
6. did neglect (or refuse) to stop the vehicle (or to make the vehicle proceed in a particular line of traffic or to make the vehicle keep to a particular line of traffic or to proceed to a particular point) 7. when directed so to do by the police constable (or the traffic warden) in the execution of his or her duty.

(B) MEANING OF TERMS

■ **1. 'That you'**

The identity of the person driving or propelling the vehicle.

■ **2. 'being the person driving (or propelling)'**

'Propelling' means that vehicles other than mechanically pro-pelled are included, such as pedal cycles.

■ **3. 'a vehicle, namely a ....'**

■ **4. 'where a police constable (or a traffic warden) was for the time being engaged in the regulation of traffic'**

This offence cannot be committed where the constable or traffic warden is not engaged in the regulation of traffic. This duty is derived from the constable's common law duty to act in protec-tion of life and property. Therefore, refusing to proceed to a census point (or a traffic survey being carried out on or in the vicinity of a road) is now an offence under this section.

■ **5. 'on a road called ....'**

See Glossary.

■ **6. 'did neglect (or refuse) to stop the vehicle (or to make the vehicle proceed in a particular line of traffic or to make the vehicle keep to a particular line of traffic or to proceed to a particular point)'**

This phrase means:

(a) 'neglect to stop' caters for cases where the driver does not see the constable's signal. It appears from the case decisions on this point that if the court feels that the driver should have seen the signal then the offence will be committed;

(b) 'refuse to stop' is straightforward refusal when such conduct can be proved;

(c) 'stop' apparently means to stop and remain stationary until signalled to move;

(d) 'proceed in a particular line of traffic' means eg to signal the driver etc, to join a line of traffic;

(e) 'keep to a particular line' means, for example, to continue in the line in which he is already travelling;

(f) 'proceed to a particular point' means eg to signal the driver to go from A to B or start a particular line of traffic etc.

■ **7. 'when directed to do so by the police constable (or the traffic warden) in the execution of his or her duty'**

The constable or warden should be acting with a view to protecting life or property as in point 4 of this offence. The direction or signal by the officer should be given clearly and in sufficient time for the defendant to stop. It has been held that a signal which was given with a lamp at night and which the driver failed to understand was not sufficient for proving failing to stop.

(C) USUAL METHOD OF PROVING THESE POINTS

■ **1. 'That you'** See (C)1 of offence 1.

■ **2. 'being the person driving (or propelling)'**
See (C)2 of offence 1.

■ **3. 'a vehicle, namely a ....'**
Vehicle is proved by describing it in a witness' statement.

■ **4. 'where a police constable (or a traffic warden) was for the time being engaged in the regulation of traffic'**
This point is proved by stating so in the constable's or warden's statement of evidence, eg, 'I was engaged in the regulation of traffic to allow pedestrians to cross safely'.

■ **5. 'on a road called ....'** See (C)4 of offence 1.

■ **6. 'did neglect (or refuse) to stop the vehicle (or to make the vehicle proceed in a particular line of traffic or to make the vehicle keep to a particular line of traffic or to proceed to a particular point)'**
The proving of this phrase will depend on the circumstances of each case. If there is an obvious refusal to stop the vehicle the officer should show this in his statement. The fact that the driver did not stop can be explained or whichever part of this point is applicable. If more than one officer or warden witnessed the incident it might save argument in court if a corroborative statement was made by the other witness.

■ **7. 'when directed so to do by the police constable or the traffic warden) in the execution of his or her duty'.**

This point is proved by the officer or warden describing how visible he or she was to the driver, for example, 'I was clearly visible to a driver approaching the crossroads etc… . Visibility was good, the weather was fine and the sun was not shining etc.' The officer/warden should then describe his signal in detail.

'The execution of his or her duty' is proved as at point 4 above.

(D) SUPPORTING EVIDENCE

Note 1. The vehicle need not be on a road at the time of the offence. The section only requires that the constable or warden should be on a road and a driver entering a road from a private drive in contravention of a constable's signal under this section could commit an offence.

Note 2. Under this section the constable need not be in uniform in comparison with section 163 of the Road Traffic Act 1988 which deals with the general power to stop vehicles.

Note 3. A notice of intended prosecution is required.

13. DRIVING WITHOUT A LICENCE
Section 87 Road Traffic Act 1988

(A) POINTS TO PROVE
1. That you 2. did drive 3. a motor vehicle, namely a .... 4. on a road called .... 5. otherwise than in accordance with a licence 6. authorising you to drive a vehicle of that class.

(B) MEANING OF TERMS
■ 1. 'That you'
Means the person driving the motor vehicle, ie his identity.

■ **2. 'did drive'**
See Glossary.
■ **3. 'a motor vehicle, namely a ....'**
See Glossary.
■ **4. 'on a road called ....'**
See Glossary.
■ **5. 'otherwise than in accordance with a licence'**
This was once difficult for the prosecution to prove as there were numerous local taxation offices which issued driving licences. Therefore the use of the so-called 'negative averment' was required. In practice it would be almost impossible to disprove a claim by the defendant that he had a licence but had lost it and had forgotten from which local taxation office it had been issued. In such a case where the true facts can only be known by the defence, the prosecution could aver that the driver was unlicensed. Since the DVLA at Swansea became responsible for driving licences the use of the negative averment for driving licences has ended but could still be used for certificates of insurance and test certificates etc.
■ **6. 'authorising you to drive a vehicle of that class'**
'Class' of vehicle shall be construed as reference to a class defined or described by reference to any characteristics of the vehicles or to any other circumstances whatsoever (section 192(3) Road Traffic Act 1988).

These different 'classes' include motor bicycle; motor tricycle; motor car; goods vehicles; motor vehicles having over eight but under 17 seats (in addition to the driver); agricultural tractors and mopeds.

(C) USUAL METHODS OF PROVING POINTS
■ **1. 'That you'**
See (C)1 of offence 1.
■ **2. 'did drive'**
See (C)2 of offence 1.

■ **3. 'a motor vehicle namely a ....'**
See (C)3 of offence 1.
■ **4. 'on a road called ....'**
See (C)4 of offence 1.
■ **5. 'otherwise than in accordance with a licence'**
In most cases the suspected driver will either say he has no licence or he will elect to produce a licence and fail to do so. Therefore, questions put to the defendant such as, 'Have you ever passed a Ministry of Transport test for this class of vehicle?' and/or, 'Do you hold or have you ever held a driving licence for this class of vehicle?' should prove useful. Note the use of a 'negative averment' as at (B)5 of this offence.
■ **6. 'authorising you to drive a vehicle of that class'**
Nine times out of 10 the vehicle concerned will be a motor bike or a motor car. But it is important to be able to classify the different types of mechanically propelled vehicles in order to be able to prove to a court in which class a vehicle falls.

(D) SUPPORTING EVIDENCE

It will assist the court if the reason for not having a licence can be mentioned in evidence. This can be done by putting a suitable question to the defendant and recording his reply.

The majority of offenders against this offence say that they forgot to renew their licence, which does not diminish their liability for this absolute offence (ie not requiring any guilty knowledge or *mens rea*). This type of contravention of the offence will be gradually phased out by the new 'life' licences, although such offences could be committed by 70-year-olds (whose licences are renewable every three years), provisional licence holders on expiry of such a licence and people suffering from certain disabilities who can only hold licences for restricted periods.

In a small number of cases the defendant will have deliberately driven without a licence. The reasons may be because he cannot pass a test; he is too young; he is a visitor to Britain, or he is a new resident who has been here for more than 12 months and can no longer drive on his foreign licence (and therefore has to pass a British driving test). Such knowledge on the part of the defendant should be proved to the court as the sentence will usually be heavier.

Note 1. It could be unlawful to act as a steersman without a driving licence, see Glossary.

Note 2. Statutory exemptions are provided in section 88 of the Road Traffic Act 1988 and, *inter alia*, allow a person to drive without a licence or cause or permit another to do so if the driver has held or is entitled to obtain a licence for that class of vehicle and an application for such a licence has been received including in it the date he was driving.

14. FAILING TO DISPLAY 'L' PLATES
Regulation 15 Motor Vehicles (Driving Licences) Regulations 1996

(A) POINTS TO PROVE
1. That you 2. being a person to whom a provisional licence to drive a motor vehicle had been granted 3. failed to comply with a condition subject to which it was granted in that 4. you drove (or rode) 5. on a road called .... 6. a motor vehicle, namely a .... 7. without there being displayed in such a manner as to be clearly visible to other persons using the road from within a reasonable distance from the front and back of the vehicle 8. 'L' plates (or 'D' plates in Wales) in the prescribed form.

(B) MEANING OF TERMS
■ 1. 'That you'
Means the person driving the motor vehicle, ie identify the driver.

■ **2. 'being a person to whom a provisional licence to drive a motor vehicle had been granted'**
Means that the defendant must be issued with a current provisional licence for the class of vehicle he was driving or riding.

■ **3. 'failed to comply with the conditions subject to which it was granted'**
Means that one of the conditions of the provisional licence has not been complied with, ie failing to display 'L' plates in this case (or 'D' plates in Wales).

■ **4. 'you drove (or rode)'** See Glossary.

■ **5. 'on a road called ....'** See Glossary.

■ **6. 'a motor vehicle, namely a ....'**
See Glossary.

■ **7. 'without being displayed in such a manner as to be clearly visible to other persons using the road from within a reasonable distance from the front and back of the vehicle'**
This element means that the 'L' plate must be unobscured by articles, dirt, snow etc, kept straight, and not wrapped around the forks of the motor bike or the bumper bar of a car etc.

■ **8. '"L" plates in the prescribed form ("D" plates in Wales)'.**
The prescribed form states that the plates should be a white 178mm (7in) square with a red letter 'L' thereon, 102mm (4in) high, 89mm (3.5in) wide and 40mm (1.5in) thick (with similar specification for the optional 'D' plate in Wales). Note that though the 'D' plate may be displayed in Wales, this should be replaced with an 'L' on driving into England.

(C) USUAL METHODS OF PROVING THESE POINTS
■ **1. 'That you'**
See (C)1 of offence 1.

■ **2. 'being a person to whom a provisional licence to drive a motor vehicle had been granted'**
This is usually proved by the police officer in the case examining

the current provisional licence. He can simply state in evidence that he examined the licence and found it to be a current provisional. The details of the licence must be recorded in the pocket book and are usually required in a statement.

A question to the effect, 'Have you any other licence for this vehicle or have you ever passed a Department of Transport test for this vehicle?' can be put to the defendant and entered in the officer's statement of evidence together with the negative reply. Should the reply be in the affirmative then the offence would not be committed.

■ 3. 'failed to comply with a condition subject to which it was granted'
This element is proved by outlining the fact that 'L' plates were not displayed as required by law.

■ 4. 'you drove (or rode)' See (C)2 of offence 1.

■ 5. 'on a road called ....' See (C)4 of offence 1.

■ 6. 'a motor vehicle, namely a ....'
See (C)3 of offence 1.

■ 7. 'without there being displayed in such a manner as to be clearly visible to other persons using the road from within a reasonable distance from the front and back of the vehicle'
The police officer's evidence is required to the effect that 'L' plates were not displayed in such a manner as to be clearly visible. For example, both 'L' plates were missing, one of the two was missing, that the white surround had been cut off, that the 'L' plates were torn, dirty or otherwise illegible. Mitigation can be provided for the defendant if evidence is given that bits of string or sticky tape showed where 'L' plates had been fitted.

■ 8. 'L' plates in the prescribed form'.
Proof is required that the size, shape or colour were not as prescribed or that there were no 'L' plates or only one displayed. Note that the Welsh alternative to the 'L' plates, the 'D' plate, is permitted in Wales.

(D) SUPPORTING EVIDENCE

Note. Generally the offence is straightforward as outlined, but if an unlicensed pillion passenger on a motor bicycle persuaded the rider to take off his 'L' plates, or the passenger took them off himself, he would aid and abet the rider's offence of no 'L' plates. The motive behind this action is usually to reduce the chances of a police check of two on a motor bicycle. Such checks are frequent where there are two on a motor bicycle with 'L' plates.

15. PROVISIONAL LICENCE HOLDER UNACCOMPANIED

Regulation 15 Motor Vehicles (Driving Licences) Regulations 1996

(A) POINTS TO PROVE
   1. - 6. (as offence 14) 7. being a class or description which he was authorised to drive by virtue of the provisional licence; 8. otherwise than under the supervision; 9. of a qualified driver; 10. who was present with him in or on the vehicle.

(B) MEANING OF TERMS
■ 1. - 6. As offence 14
■ 7. As offence 14 'being a class or description which he was authorised to drive by virtue of a provisional licence'
The class or description of the motor vehicle when the provisional licence holder is required to be accompanied is as shown in his provisional licence.
■ 8. 'otherwise than under the supervision'
It is a question of fact in each case whether or not the qualified driver was supervising. The duty of the supervisor is to prevent

the learner from acting unskillfully or carelessly or in a manner likely to cause danger to others. If the 'qualified driver' does not do what can be reasonably expected of him regarding these duties the learner could be said to be not under supervision.

■ 9. 'of a qualified driver'

The supervisor must be a 'qualified driver' as defined by regulation 13 of the Motor Vehicles (Driving Licences) Regulations 1996, namely, a person who holds a full licence authorising him to drive as a full licence holder a motor vehicle of the same class or description as the vehicle being driven by the holder of the provisional licence; who is at least 21 years of age and who has held a full licence for at least three years.

■ 10. 'who was present with him in or on the vehicle'.

The learner cannot argue that he was being correctly supervised by someone standing on the footpath or in radio contact with him etc, the supervisor must be in or on the vehicle at all times.

(C) USUAL METHOD OF PROVING THESE POINTS

■ 1. to 6. as offence 14.

■ 7. 'being a class or description which he was authorised to drive by virtue of a provisional licence'

By showing in the police officer's statement of evidence that the provisional licence he held covered the class of vehicle he was driving. If not authorised to drive the class in question the correct offence would be driving without a licence (offence 13).

■ 8. 'otherwise than under the supervision'

The most usual way of proving this point will be that the learner was alone in the vehicle. Occasionally he will be accompanied by a 'qualified driver' but because such person was asleep, drunk or poorly etc, the learner would not be classed as being supervised. The observations of a witness or an admission by the accused would prove this point.

■ 9. 'of a qualified driver'

This point is proved by examining the details of the licence of anyone accompanying the learner to see if the licence complies with the definition of qualified driver at (B)9 of this offence. If it does there is no offence. A police officer can demand the production of the driving licence of a 'qualified driver' under the Road Traffic Act.

■ **10. 'who was present with him or on the vehicle'.**
This is proved as at (C)8 of this offence, inasmuch as the learner will be alone in the vehicle.

(D) SUPPORTING EVIDENCE

Note 1. A supervisor can aid and abet the learner to drive while over the prescribed limit etc. A conviction ensued where the supervisor had been drinking with the driver who was seen to swerve from side to side (*Crampton v Fish* (1969) 113 SJ 1003).
Note 2. A US forces' driving permit is not sufficient to allow supervision (*Urey v Lummis* [1962] 2 All ER 463) as a 'licence' means a licence to drive a motor vehicle granted under Part III of the Road Traffic Act 1988.

16. PROVISIONAL LICENCE HOLDER CARRYING PASSENGER ON A MOTOR BIKE
Regulation 15 Motor Vehicles (Driving Licences) Regulations 1996

(A) POINTS TO PROVE
1. - 6. as offence 14; 7. and not having attached thereto a sidecar 8. while carrying on it a passenger.

(B) MEANING OF TERMS
■ **1. to 6.** as offence 14.
■ **7. 'and not having attached thereto a sidecar'**
A flat tubular framework attached to a motor bicycle with a

wheel on an axle welded to that framework is not a sidecar for this purpose (*Cox v Harrison* [1968] 3 All ER 811). In *Keen v Parker* [1976] RTR 213 it was held that a sidecar designed for the carriage of goods was just as much a sidecar as one which carried passengers.

■ **8. 'while carrying on it a person who was not a qualified driver'.**

'Qualified driver' is defined at (B)9 of offence 15.

(C) USUAL METHOD OF PROVING THESE POINTS

■ **1. - 6.** as offence 14.

■ **7. 'and not having attached thereto a sidecar'**

In the majority of this type of offence there will not be a sidecar fitted. But in a few cases careful evidence must be gathered to show whether the attachment falls within *Cox v Harrison* at (B)7 above. A sketch plan may prove helpful.

■ **8. 'while carrying on it a passenger'.**

There must be evidence, usually of the police officer's observations, that there was a pillion passenger.

(D) SUPPORTING EVIDENCE

If it can be proved that the pillion passenger knew the driver was only a learner, the passenger would most likely commit the offence of aiding and abetting the learner to carry a passenger.

17. DRIVING WITH EXCESS ALCOHOL

Section 5(1) Road Traffic Act 1988

(A) POINTS TO PROVE

1. That you 2. did drive (or attempt to drive or were in charge of) 3. a certain motor vehicle, namely .... 4. on a road (or public place) called .... 5. after consuming so much alcohol that the proportion thereof in your breath (blood or urine) exceeds the prescribed limit.

(B) MEANING OF TERMS
■ 1. 'That you'
Means the person driving over the prescribed limit, ie the identity of the driver.
■ 2. 'did drive (or attempt to drive or were in charge of)'
'Attempting to drive' means that there must be an act substantially close to actually driving. Acts such as trying to start the engine, or a person who is sitting in the driving seat trying to put the vehicle in gear or 'revving up' the engine (even though the clutch had burnt out) *(R v Farrance* [1978] Crim LR 496) are examples of 'attempting to drive', provided there is an immediate intention of driving.

'In charge of' means that once a person takes a vehicle on a road or public place he normally remains in charge of that vehicle until he has taken it off the road or public place again. He will cease to be in charge where some intervening act occurs to remove the responsibility for being in charge from him. An example would be where someone else takes charge of the vehicle to such a degree that he will not resume control of the vehicle, such as where he gives his friend the ignition key and a taxi is ordered to take him home.
■ 3. 'a certain motor vehicle, namely ....'
See Glossary.
■ 4. 'on a road (or public place) called ....'
See Glossary for 'road'.

'Public place' means any place to which the public have access, eg a farmer's field near a race course which is used for parking purposes on race days. This is so notwithstanding that the field could be closed at any time and that certain people could be refused admission. Generally a place is public if the majority of the public have access to it.

A place is private and this offence cannot be committed where only a minority group of the public are admitted. For example where a field leading to a river could only be used, according to a sign, for 'Parking - Members of the Walton Angling Club only', it would constitute a private field. If the sign said 'Parking - No Caravans', a restricted class cannot use the field, but as the majority group could use it the field would be a public place.

■ **5. 'after consuming so much alcohol that the proportion thereof in your breath (blood or urine) exceeds the prescribed limit'.**

The prescribed limits at present are:

(a) 35 microgrammes of alcohol in 100 millilitres of breath;

(b) 80 milligrammes of alcohol in 100 millilitres of blood;

(c) 107 milligrammes of alcohol in 100 millilitres of urine.

(C) USUAL METHODS OF PROVING THESE POINTS

■ **1. 'That you'**

See (C)1 of offence 1.

■ **2. 'did drive (or attempt to drive or was in charge of)'**

See (C)2 of offence 1 for 'drive'.

'Attempt to drive' can be proved by the officer in the case or another witness who saw the defendant attempting to drive. An admission on the part of the defendant would also help the prosecution case. Failing an admission a question to the defendant such as, 'Where did you intend to go when you got into your car?' or, 'What were you trying to do?' etc, may help to prove that he had an intention to drive as discussed at point (B)2 of this offence. The precise details of the evidence of attempting to drive that the officer or other witness saw must be shown in their statements of evidence.

'In charge of' can be proved by the police officer or other witness who saw him near or sitting in the vehicle for example. Questions to determine whether he had taken any steps to prevent him driving may be necessary, such as, 'Where are the ignition keys?' or, 'Is anybody else in charge of this vehicle?' See (D) of this offence for the statutory defence to being in charge.

■ **3. 'a certain motor vehicle, namely ....'**
See (C)3 of offence 1.

■ **4. 'on a road (or public place) called ....'**
See (C)4 of offence 1 for 'road'. To prove whether a place is 'public' could necessitate taking a statement from a person who had authorised access to a normally private place; enquiring about and keeping observations on the place to show actual usage; or describing any permanent or temporary signs that relate to who had access.

■ **5. 'after consuming so much alcohol the proportion thereof in your breath (blood or urine) exceeds the prescribed limit'.**
Evidence of the proportion of alcohol in a specimen of breath, blood or urine may be by a document which is:

(a) a statement automatically produced by the breath analysis machine by which the proportion of alcohol in the breath specimen was measured and a certificate signed by a constable that the statement relates to a specimen provided by the accused at the date and time shown in the statement; and

(b) a certificate signed by an authorised analyst.

Where an analyst's findings are challenged by the defence, the prosecution could call the analyst to give evidence to explain his findings to the court.

(D) SUPPORTING EVIDENCE

Most police forces have produced a pro-forma to lead the officer in charge of the case through the procedure. The majority of these forms have been in use since October 1967 when the drink/driving law regarding being over the prescribed limit (OPL) was introduced. The forms have been found to work well in practice. The necessity for long entries in the constable's pocket book has been eliminated.

The general idea with pro-formas is that they should be filled in as the procedure progresses in order to qualify as 'notes made at the time'. Such notes can be used to refresh memories and it has been found that a most accurate record of the investigation of OPL offences can thus be obtained.

Note 1. It is a defence for a person charged with 'Being in Charge' to prove that at the time he is alleged to have committed the offence the circumstances were such that there was no likelihood of his driving the vehicle while the proportion of alcohol in his breath, blood or urine remained likely to exceed the prescribed limit. However, in determining whether there was such a likelihood the court may disregard any injury to him and any damage to the vehicle.

The last part of this defence means that just because driving was impossible because of injury to him or damage to the vehicle, the court will not automatically find him not guilty. The court can disregard any injury or damage and still find that he was in charge of the vehicle. Note however that if a wheel clamp is fitted, this cannot be disregarded by the court as amounting to 'damage to the vehicle' (*Drake v DPP* [1994] Crim LR 855).

Note 2. A supervisor can aid and abet the learner to drive while over the prescribed limit etc. A conviction ensued where the supervisor had been drinking with the driver who was seen to swerve from side to side (*Crampton v Fish* (1969) 113 SJ 1003).

Note 3. Also consider, where appropriate, the offence of driving, attempting to drive or being in charge of a motor vehicle on a road or public place while unfit to drive through drink or drugs. 'Drugs' include any intoxicant other than alcohol, therefore even solvent abuse may be covered by this offence.

Note 4. The offence of obstructing the police under section 89(2) of the Police Act 1996 may be appropriate where the accused deliberately obstructs the police in the execution of their duty.

18. FAILURE TO WEAR A SEAT BELT

Regulation 5 of the Motor Vehicles (Wearing of Seat Belts) Regulations 1993 and section 14 of the Road Traffic Act 1988

(A) POINTS TO PROVE

1. That you 2. did drive/were a passenger 3. in a motor vehicle 4. on a road 5. whilst not wearing a prescribed type of adult belt.

(B) MEANING OF TERMS

■ 1. 'That you'

Means the person driving or the passenger, ie the identity and not being a person under the age of 14 years.

■ 2. 'Did drive/were a passenger'

Passenger means carried in the vehicle, ie riding in the front seat of a motor vehicle (other than a two wheeled motor cycle with or without a sidecar) or riding in the rear seat of a motor car or a passenger car which is not a motor car.

■ 3. 'In a motor vehicle' (which is not a two wheeled motor cycle with or without sidecar)

See Glossary for 'motor vehicle'.

■ 4. 'on a road' See Glossary.

■ 5. 'while not wearing a prescribed type of adult belt'.

This point means a seat belt as defined, ie in these Regulations, 'adult belt' means a seat belt in respect of which one or more of the following requirements is satisfied, namely, that:

(a) it is a three-point belt which has been marked in accordance with regulation 47(7) of the Construction and Use Regulations;

(b) it is a lap belt which has been so marked;

(c) it is a seat belt that falls within regulation 47(4)(c)(i) or (ii) of those Regulations;

(d) it is a seat belt fitted in a relevant vehicle ('the vehicle in question') and comprised in a restraint system -

(i) of a type which has been approved by an authority of another Member State for use by all persons who are either aged 13 years or more or of 150cm or more in height, and

(ii) in respect of which, by virtue of such approval, the requirements of the law of another Member State corresponding to these Regulations would be met were it to be worn by persons who are either aged 13 years or more or of 150 centimetres or more in height when travelling in the vehicle in question in that State.

The interpretation of references to relevant vehicles:

(1) In these Regulations 'relevant vehicle' means -

    (a) a passenger car,

    (b) a light goods vehicle, or

    (c) a small bus.

(2) For the purposes of this regulation -

'light goods vehicle' means a goods vehicle which -

    (a) has four or more wheels,

    (b) has a maximum design speed exceeding 25km per hour,

    (c) has a maximum laden weight not exceeding 3.5 tonnes;

'small bus' means a motor vehicle which -

    (a) is constructed or adapted for use for the carriage of passengers and is not a goods vehicle,

    (b) has more than 8 seats in addition to the driver's seat,

    (c) has four or more wheels,

    (d) has a maximum design speed exceeding 25km per hour,

    (e) has a maximum laden weight not exceeding 3.5 tonnes,

    (f) is not constructed or adapted for the carriage of standing passengers.

(C) USUAL METHODS OF PROVING THESE POINTS

■ **1. 'That you'** See (C)1 of offence 1.

■ **2. 'did drive/were a passenger'**

These points can be proved by the police officer's observations in his statement of evidence.

■ **3. 'in a motor vehicle'**
See (C)3 of offence 1.

■ **4. 'on a road'**
See Glossary.

■ **5. 'while not wearing a prescribed type of adult belt'.**
This point can be proved in the majority of cases by the observations of the reporting officer.

Where there is any doubt as to whether the seat belt is as prescribed, regulation 47 of the Construction and Use Regulations will have to be consulted.

Normally the following sentence in the reporting officer's statement will suffice: 'The seat belt was fitted and was in good working order when I tested it. I saw that the driver (passenger) was not wearing it.'

(D) SUPPORTING EVIDENCE

Note 1. Be aware of the following exemptions in regulation 6.
(1) The requirements of regulation 5 do not apply to:
    (a)   a person holding a medical certificate;
    (b)   a person using a vehicle constructed or adapted for the delivery of goods or mail to consumers or addresses, as the case may be, while engaged in making local rounds of deliveries or collections;
    (c)   a person driving a vehicle while performing a manoeuvre which includes reversing;
    (d)   a qualified driver (within the meaning given by regulation 13 of the Motor Vehicles (Driving Licences) Regulations 1996) who is supervising the holder of a provisional licence (within the meaning of Part III of the Act) while that holder is performing a manoeuvre which includes reversing;
    (e)   a person by whom, as provided in the Motor Vehicles (Driving Licences) Regulations 1996, a test of competence to drive is being conducted and his wearing a seat

belt would endanger himself or any other person;

(f) a person driving or riding in a vehicle while it is being used for fire brigade or police purposes or for carrying a person in lawful custody (a person who is being so carried being included in this exemption);

(g) the driver of -
(i) a licensed taxi while it is being used for seeking hire, or answering a call for hire, or carrying a passenger for hire, or
(ii) a private hire vehicle while it is being used to carry a passenger for hire;

(h) a person riding in a vehicle being used under a trade licence, for the purpose of investigating or remedying a mechanical fault in the vehicle;

(j) a disabled person who is wearing a disabled person's belt; or

(k) a person riding in a vehicle while it is taking part in a procession organised by or on behalf of the Crown.

(2) Without prejudice to paragraph (1)(k), the requirements of regulation 5 do not apply to a person riding in a vehicle which is taking part in a procession held to mark or commemorate an event if either:

(a) the procession is one commonly or customarily held in the police area or areas in which it is being held; or

(b) notice in respect of the procession was given in accordance with section 11 of the Public Order Act 1986.

(3) The requirements of regulation 5 do not apply to:

(a) a person driving a vehicle if the driver's seat is not provided with an adult belt;

(b) a person riding in the front of a vehicle if no adult belt is available for him in the front of the vehicle;

(c) a person riding in the rear of a vehicle if no adult belt is available for him in the rear of the vehicle.

Also see Schedule 2 of these Regulations for further interpretation re availability of seat belts.

Note 2. The seat belt law for children (under the age of 14) can be found at section 15 Road Traffic Act 1988, the Motor Vehicles (Wearing of Seat Belts) Regulations 1993 and the Motor Vehicles (Wearing of Seat Belts by Children in Front Seats) Regulations 1993. Where a child (under 14) is a front seat or a rear seat passenger (providing a rear seat belt is fitted) **the driver will commit an offence** unless the child is wearing a seat belt conforming with the Regulations.

19. DANGEROUS PARTS
Regulation 100(1) Road Vehicles (Construction and Use) Regulations 1986, and section 40A Road Traffic Act 1988

(A) POINTS TO PROVE
1. That you 2. did use (or cause, or permit to be used) 3. on a road called .... 4. a certain motor vehicle namely a .... (or trailer drawn by a motor vehicle) 5. a part (or accessory) of which, namely .... (specify) 6. was in such condition, that danger was caused 7. or was likely to be caused to persons in or on that vehicle (or trailer) or on a road in that .... (specify defect).

(B) MEANING OF TERMS
■ 1. 'That you'
Means the identity of the person using, causing or permitting the use of the motor vehicle.
■ 2. 'did use (or cause, or permit to be used)'
See Glossary.
■ 3. 'on a road called ....' See Glossary.
■ 4. 'a certain motor vehicle namely a ....' (or trailer drawn by a motor vehicle).
See See Glossary for 'motor vehicle' and 'trailer'.

■ 5. 'a part (or accessory) of which ....'

Means that such things as doors, windows and wings are parts, and such things as wing mirrors, windscreen wipers and roof racks are accessories.

A tow chain has been held not to be a 'part' (*Jenkins v Deane* (1933) 103 LJKB 250), but a tow bar connecting a vehicle and a trailer together has been held to come within the regulation where the joining was defective (*O'Neill v Brown* [1961] 1 QB 420).

■ 6. 'was in such condition, that danger was caused'

This point means that the condition caused danger or in other words injured someone. For example where a hole appears in the wing of a car and a pedestrian is cut by the sharp rusty edges of the hole, then danger is caused.

In *Reeve v Webb* (1972) 117 SJ 127 it was held that alterations to exhaust pipes fall within another part of this regulation.

■ 7. 'or was likely to be caused to persons in or on that vehicle (or trailer) or on a road in that .... (specify defect)'.

'Likely to be caused' means potentially dangerous. Examples would be sharp edges jutting from the body of a motor vehicle; a loose driver's seat which could lead to loss of control of the vehicle; projecting wheel wing nuts or mudguards which could strike a pedestrian; a loose rear bumper which may fall off and cause an accident.

'To persons in or on that vehicle (or trailer)' means that the danger or potential danger is sufficient if it applies to passengers or even the driver of the motor vehicle concerned.

'Or on a road' covers potential danger or actual danger to pedestrians or anyone not actually in or on the offending motor vehicle.

'In that .... (specify defect)' means that the offence must show what parts and accessories are not maintained in good condition (*Simmons v Fowler* (1950) 48 LGR 623).

(C) USUAL METHODS OF PROVING THESE POINTS

■ **1. 'That you'**
See (C)1 of offence 1.

■ **2. 'did use (or cause, or permit to be used)'**
See (C)2 of offence 5.

In the case of 'use' for construction and use offences there is an absolute prohibition on the part of the employer. If an offence is committed and the employer was quite unaware of any defect he is still liable for 'using' (*Green v Burnett* [1954] 3 All ER 273). Therefore, to prove the offence of using against the employer as well as against the driver, the employer must be interviewed and questioned as follows:

'Are you (or your firm) the owner of motor vehicle ....?'
Then, 'Was the vehicle being used on your (or your firm's) business at ..... (time) ..... on ..... (date) ..... in ..... (road) .....?'

For the offence of 'using' these questions must receive the answer 'Yes'. While it is not necessary to prove the employer knew of any defect it is good evidence for the prosecution if he admits he did.

■ **3. 'on a road called ....'** See (C)4 of offence 1.

■ **4. 'a certain motor vehicle namely a ....' (or trailer drawn by a motor vehicle)'** See (C)3 of offence 1.

■ **5. 'a part (or accessory) of which, namely ....' (specify)**
This point can be proved by the police officer dealing with the case describing the item in question in his statement of evidence, eg, 'The front nearside wing was badly corroded .... etc'. Specific details of the defective parts and/or accessories must be given in the charge and therefore in the prosecution evidence (*Simmons v Fowler* (1950) 48 LGR 623).

■ **6. 'was in such condition, that danger was caused'**
This point is proved, firstly by the prosecution witness (most likely the police officer) examining the personal injury and describing it in his evidence. Secondly, a statement from the injured party detailing the injury and how it was caused would be required.

■ 7. 'or was likely to be caused to persons in or on that vehicle (or trailer) or on a road in that .... (specify defect).

Where no injury is caused, the above element has to be proved. This is usually done by the subjective judgment of the officer concerned. Namely, a sentence in the police officer's statement of evidence to the effect that 'Should anyone come into contact with the jagged metal on the front nearside wing they would be injured', or, 'If a pedestrian collided with the piece of metal left after the front nearside wing mirror had broken off, he would be injured'. The court will then use its judgment regarding the proof of potential danger.

(D) SUPPORTING EVIDENCE

Note. Several other offences are included in the above Regulations but are not quite so common as the offence outlined. The other offences include the number and manner of carrying of passengers being dangerous or potentially dangerous; insecure or dangerous load; and using a motor vehicle for an unsuitable purpose.

20. DEFECTIVE BRAKES

Regulation 18 Road Vehicles (Construction and Use) Regulations 1986 and section 41A Road Traffic Act 1988

(A) POINTS TO PROVE

1. That you 2. did use (or cause or permit to be used) 3. on a road called .... 4. a motor vehicle, namely a .... (or trailer) 5. on which a part of (the means of operation of) the braking system fitted thereto 6. was not maintained in good and efficient working order and properly adjusted.

(B) MEANING OF TERMS

■ 1. 'That you'

Means the identity of the person using, causing or permitting the use.

■ 2. 'did use (or cause or permit to be used)'

See Glossary.

■ 3. 'on a road called' See Glossary.

■ 4. 'a motor vehicle, namely a .... (or trailer)'

See Glossary for 'motor vehicle' and 'trailer'.

■ 5. 'on which a part of (the means of operation of) the braking system fitted thereto'

This point means that 'a part', eg the brake shoes or brake pads were not maintained and/or the 'means of operation' such as the hand brake lever ratchet or the cable (if fitted) was not maintained. It was held in *Kennett v British Airports Authority* [1975] Crim LR 106 that every part of the braking system and of the means of operation must be maintained etc. Note that a brake drum is part of the wheel and not the braking system.

■ 6. 'was not maintained in good efficient working order and properly adjusted'.

This point means an absolute requirement for a person to maintain his brakes to escape liability. It is insufficient to show that the brakes were regularly maintained. 'Not maintained' usually includes worn, seized or rusted parts etc and 'not properly adjusted' includes stretched cables or inoperative self-adjusting ratchets on drum brakes etc.

(C) USUAL METHODS OF PROVING THESE POINTS

■ 1. 'That you' See (C)1 of offence 1.

■ 2. 'did use (or cause or permit to be used)'

See (C)2 of offence 5.

In the case of 'use' for construction and use offences see (C)2 of offence 19.

■ **3. 'on a road called ....'**

See (C)4 of offence 1.

■ **4. 'a motor vehicle, namely a .... (or trailer)'**

See (C)3 of offence 1.

■ **5. 'on which a part of (the means of operation of) the braking system, fitted thereto'**

This point can be proved by showing the brakes don't work by using a simple test such as pushing the vehicle along the road with the brake(s) set. If a vehicle examiner who has been authorised by a chief constable examines the brakes his evidence will show a more detailed inspection and will probably name the 'part' concerned.

Note that an officer who is not authorised to test and inspect will have to ask the driver before carrying out his examination. If permission is refused he can hold the vehicle until an authorised examiner arrives where he feels it would be dangerous for the vehicle to proceed. If the driver still refuses to wait he commits a further possible offence, but there is no power to detain or 'arrest' the vehicle.

■ **6. 'was not maintained in good and efficient working order and properly adjusted'.**

This point is proved along with the last point. Obviously defective parts such as broken brake cable, leaking hydraulic fluid, or a handbrake that won't catch on its ratchet etc, can be proved by the observations of almost anyone. Where an accident is caused by alleged brake failure, or other more technical circumstances arise, the services of a trained vehicle examiner may be required. The most common brake defects are worn shoes and pads, seized cylinders and poor adjustment. In *Stoneley v Richardson* [1973] RTR 229 it was held that defective brakes do not have to be proved by an authorised examiner. Provided the defendant consents to the test or inspection the person examining the brakes (usually a constable) does not need to be an authorised examiner.

Inefficiency etc is sometimes proved by the use of an instrument which measures braking efficiency, called a Tapley meter.

(D) SUPPORTING EVIDENCE

A practical consideration when testing vehicle parts is for the defendant to be asked to operate the part, such as brakes, himself. In this way an allegation to the effect that the officer did not apply the brake correctly may be quickly dealt with by saying, 'After (the officer) tested the brakes and found the handbrake to be defective I asked the defendant to apply the handbrake. He did so but could not get it to work.'

Note 1. A latent defect amounting to a dangerous condition is not a defence but would be good mitigation, *F Austin (Leyton) Ltd v East* [1961] Crim LR 119. The facts of this case showed that there was no negligence but nevertheless such offences are absolute.

21. DEFECTIVE WINDSCREEN WIPERS
Regulation 34(6) Road Vehicles (Construction and Use) Regulations 1986 and section 42 of the Road Traffic Act 1988

(A) POINTS TO PROVE
1. That you 2. did use (or cause or permit to be used) 3. on a road called .... 4. a motor vehicle, namely a .... 5. on which the windscreen wiper was not maintained in good and efficient working order, and/or properly adjusted.

(B) MEANING OF TERMS
■ 1. 'That you'
Means the person's identity.

■ **2. 'did use (or cause or permit to be used)'**
See Glossary.

■ **3. 'on a road called ....'** See Glossary.

■ **4. 'a motor vehicle, namely a ....'**
See Glossary.

■ **5. 'on which the windscreen wiper was not maintained in good and efficient working order and/or properly adjusted'.**

The point means that the switch, the motor or the arms or blades were defective or missing etc. Common faults are wiper blades missing or the electric motor failing.

(C) USUAL METHODS OF PROVING THESE POINTS
■ **1. 'That you'**
See (C)1 of offence 1.

■ **2. 'did use (or cause or permit to be used)'**
See (C)2 of offences 5 and 19.

3. 'on a road called ....' See (C)4 of offence 1.

■ **4. 'a motor vehicle, namely a ....'**
See (C)3 of offence 1.

■ **5. 'on which the windscreen wiper was not maintained in good and efficient working order and/or properly adjusted'.**

This point can be proved simply by testing the wipers and getting no response. Where the motor is working the offence can still be committed where the arm or blade is missing. The defendant should also be asked to operate the wipers to avoid allegations to the effect that the wipers were not switched on correctly.

(D) SUPPORTING EVIDENCE

Note 1. Depending on the make of motor vehicle, normally there are two wipers fitted and both must work as regulation 34(1) of the above regulation insists that 'an adequate view of the road in front of the near and offsides of the vehicle…' is required. But this is the general position and in vehicles like Minis it could be argued that such a view can be obtained when only the wiper in front of the driver works, therefore each vehicle must be dealt with separately.

Note 2. Regulation 34(1) states that if a view to the front can be obtained without looking through the windscreen, wipers are not required. Only old vehicles pre about 1940 and the occasional newer vehicle such as some Land Rovers have the front opening windscreens.

22. DEFECTIVE SILENCER

Regulation 54(1) Road Vehicles (Construction and Use) Regulations 1986 and section 42 of the Road Traffic Act 1988

(A) POINTS TO PROVE

1. That you 2. did use (or cause or permit to be used) 3. on a road called .... 4. a vehicle propelled by an internal combustion engine, namely a .... 5. so that the exhaust gases from the engine escaped into the atmosphere without first passing through the silencer, expansion chamber or other contrivance required to be fitted by the Motor Vehicles (Construction and Use) Regulations.

(B) MEANING OF TERMS

■ 1. 'That you'
Means the identity of the person using the motor vehicle etc.

■ 2. 'did use (or cause or permit to be used)'
See Glossary.

■ 3. 'on a road called ....'
See Glossary.

■ **4. a vehicle propelled by an internal combustion engine, namely a ....'**

See Glossary.

As the majority of vehicles are propelled in this manner, this point speaks for itself.

■ **5. 'so that the exhaust gases from the engine escaped into the atmosphere without first passing through the silencer, expansion chamber or other contrivance required to be fitted by the Motor Vehicles (Construction and Use) Regulations'**

This point means for example that the gases from the engine escape from the faulty manifold (which is at the exit point adjacent to the engine) or a broken front pipe, a broken expansion chamber or from the silencer (provided this occurs before they pass through it). These regulations require that either a silencer, expansion chamber or other contrivance is fitted as may be reasonable to reduce the noise. If an exhaust system has two such articles this offence is not committed if the gases pass through any such article before escaping into the atmosphere.

(C) USUAL METHODS OF PROVING THESE POINTS

■ **1. 'That you'**

See (C)1 of offence 1.

■ **2. 'did use (or cause or permit to be used)'**

See (C)2 of offences 5 and 19.

■ **3. 'on a road called ....'**

See (C)4 of offence 1.

■ **4. 'a vehicle propelled by an internal combustion engine, namely a ....'**

This point can be proved by describing the vehicle in the statement of the police officer who is dealing with the case, eg, 'I caused the defendant, John Smith to stop the Ford saloon motor car registered number .... etc'.

■ **5. 'so that the exhaust gases from the engine escaped into the atmosphere without first passing through the silencer, expansion chamber or other contrivance required to be fitted by the Motor Vehicles (Construction and Use) Regulations'.**

This point can be proved by inspecting the silencer system with the engine running and watching where the gases are escaping. In the vast majority of cases the exhaust pipe corrodes around the bend which goes over the rear axle on motor cars or that particular pipe breaks away from the end of the silencer. However, there is no offence against this regulation if only the tail pipe (ie the piece leading the gases into the atmosphere from the end of the silencer which is the furthest from the engine) is defective, as the gases will have passed through the silencer.

(D) SUPPORTING EVIDENCE

Motor cycles owners have been known to remover the baffle plates of the silencer to make the engine sound bigger and 'sporty'. A way of proving this is to push a retractable steel rule (a useful item for a police officer to carry) up the exhaust pipe and into the silencer. If the rule passes through the silencer unhindered, suitable questions could be put to the rider to prove a regulation 54(2) offence.

Note. The further offence of failing to maintain such a system is contrary to regulation 54(2) of these Regulations. This offence can be considered where a hole appears in the side of the silencer etc, as some doubt exists whether the gases have passed 'through' the silencer etc, if they have passed through half of the silencer, Until there is judicial assistance to say that such gases must pass all the way through a silencer to escape liability under regulation 54(1), a regulation 54(2) offence may be the safest offence.

23. DEFECTIVE TYRES

Regulation 27(1) (or (4)) Road Vehicles (Construction and Use) Regulations 1986 and section 41A of the Road Traffic Act 1988

(A) POINTS TO PROVE

1. That you 2. used (or caused or permitted to be used) 3. on a road called .... 4. a motor vehicle (or trailer), namely a .... 5. fitted with a pneumatic tyre 6. whose grooves of the tread pattern of the tyre did not have a depth of at least 1. 6 mm throughout a continuous band situated in the central three-quarters of the breadth of the tread and round the entire outer circumference of the tyre.

(B) MEANING OF TERMS

■ 1. 'That you'

Means the identity of the person using the motor vehicle etc.

■ 2. 'used (or caused or permitted to be used)'

■ 3. 'on a road called ....'

■ 4. 'a motor vehicle (or trailer) namely a ....'

With effect from 1 January 1992 the 'old' offences at paragraphs (f) and (g) of regulation 27(1) of the 1986 Regulations no longer apply to passenger motor cars other than motor cars constructed or adapted to carry no more than eight seated passengers in addition to the driver, or to goods vehicles with a maximum gross weight which does not exceed 3,500 kg. The new offence applies to motor cars and goods vehicles other than those shown above and also applies to light trailers first used on or after 3 January 1933, ie, a trailer with a maximum gross weight not exceeding 3,500kg.

In other words the old offences under (f) and (g) above now apply to motor cars with eight or more seats or goods vehicles 3,500 kg or under and to the other categories of vehicle not mentioned here.

The new offence under regulation 27(4)(d)(f) (which contains the same requirement of 1.6mm minimum depth throughout a continuous band of three-quarters of the breadth) applies to the vast majority of motor cars and trailers and goods vehicles of 3,500kg or under.

■ 5. 'fitted with a pneumatic tyre'

Pneumatic tyre means inflatable as opposed to the early tyre or solid tyres.

■ 6. 'whose grooves on the tread pattern did not have a depth of at least 1. 6mm throughout a continuous band situated in the central three-quarters of the breadth of the tread and round the entire outer circumference of the tyre'.

'Tread pattern' means the raised and lowered pattern which, in modern tyres, is provided around the walls of the tyre to a small degree as well as where the tyre makes contact with the road surface. 'Tread' is the part of the tyre which comes into contact with the road surface in normal driving, ie not when cornering at speed.

Therefore, this point means that the tyre did not have a 1.6mm depth of tread pattern grooves around the tyre in a continuous band situated in the central three-quarters of the width of the tread. It follows that if there is a small bald patch (or a patch with grooves less than 1.6mm deep) 4cm in diameter on a tread width of 12cm an offence is committed, for 4 cm is more than a quarter of the 12cm width of tread. It is important to note that the bald patch or the patch without the 1.6mm depth of tread grooves is not required to go right around the tyre.

It is sufficient to contravene this regulation where the patch is more than a quarter of the breadth of the tread, because there cannot be at least three-quarters of good tread around the whole circumference of the tyre in such a case.

It should be noted that the required three-quarters width of 1.6mm tread pattern grooves should be in a continuous band.

Therefore, where the tread is below 1.6mm depth in the middle of the tread and around the circumference of the tyre it is no good the defendant adding up the 'bits' on either side of the worn part to try to make a good three-quarters.

(C) USUAL METHODS OF PROVING THESE POINTS

■ 1. 'That you'
See (C)1 of offence 1.

■ 2. 'used (or caused or permitted to be used)'
See (C)2 of offences 5 and 19.

■ 3. 'on a road called ....'
See (C)4 of offence 1.

■ 4. 'a motor vehicle (or trailer), namely a ....'
Proof of the number of seats in a passenger motor car or the maximum gross weight of a goods vehicle may be necessary to show this new offence applies to the vehicle in question. For example: 'The motor car had been adapted to carry [8 - or specify] seated passengers (but not more than [8 - or specify]) in addition to the driver.' 'The goods vehicle was ....[specify weight].'

■ 5. 'fitted with a pneumatic tyre'
This point is proved by describing the tyre in question, eg, 'The front nearside tyre was a radial, such and such a make, size 165 x 14 and was designed as a tubeless tyre'. It is important for the prosecution case to try to identify the tyre by taking the tyre or batch number which will usually be something like 824927 16E, on the tyre wall in letters and figures about 1 cm high - in about a quarter of all checks the number is non-existent or illegible and the police officer should try to remember other forms of identification such as marks or scratches etc on the tyre. This precaution may well deter a dishonest defendant bringing a totally different tyre to court and alleging that the officer was mistaken as the tyre was within the law.

■ 6. 'whose grooves of the tread pattern of the tyre did not have a depth of at least 1. 6 mm throughout a continuous

band situated in the central three-quarters of the breadth of the tread and round the entire outer circumference of the tyre'.

This point is proved beyond any doubt when a completely bald patch exceeding a quarter of the breadth of the tread is present. In the other case where the depth of the tread pattern grooves is in issue an approved measuring device can be used.

(D) SUPPORTING EVIDENCE

Each tyre must be treated as a separate entity and separate informations must be laid where offences concern more than one tyre *(Saines v Woodhouse* [1970] 2 All ER 388). This includes double tyres on lorries and close coupled wheels.

Note 1. In the case of *Stoneley v Richardson* [1973] Crim LR 310 it was held that it does not matter whether or not the constable who inspected the tyre was an authorised examiner under section 67 Road Traffic Act 1988. Where the constable is not authorised the defendant could have allowed the constable to carry out the inspection.

Note 2. The further offences under regulation 27 should be considered. These are regulation 27(1) (a) to (h) with the exception of (f) and (g). Further offences include tyres not maintained in good order, with defects such as cuts, bulges, lumps, tears or exposed ply or cord; wrongly inflated tyres or tyres put to the wrong use; recut pneumatic tyres where the ply or cord has been exposed, or those recut in a pattern other than to the manufacturer's specification.

Note 3. Vehicles exceeding capacity for eight seated passengers or 3,500kg require at least 1mm of tread.

Note 4. Be aware of exempted vehicles such as agricultural trailers and pedestrian controlled works trucks.

24. QUITTING WITHOUT STOPPING ENGINE AND SETTING BRAKE

Regulation 107(1) Road Vehicles (Construction and Use) Regulations 1986, and section 42 Road Traffic Act 1988

(A) POINTS TO PROVE

1. That you 2. did cause (or permit) 3. to be on a road called .... 4. a motor vehicle, namely a .... 5. which was not attended 6. by a person duly licensed to drive it 7. without the engine being stopped and/or 8. without the parking brake being effectively set.

(B) MEANING OF TERMS

■ 1. 'That you'
Means the person quitting the vehicle.
■ 2. 'did cause (or permit)'
See Glossary.
■ 3. 'to be on a road called ....'
See Glossary.
■ 4. 'a motor vehicle, namely a ....'
See Glossary.

Notable exceptions include police, fire brigade and ambulance purposes, and vehicles which require the engine to run to operate special machinery or apparatus such as a gully emptying vehicle.

■ 5. 'which was not attended'
Means there is no person able to keep it under observation and reach it in time to prevent anything untoward happening (*Starfire Diamond Rings Ltd v Angel* (1962) 106 SJ 854 and *Ingleton of Ilford Ltd v General Accident & Co* [1967] 2 Lloyd's Rep 179).

■ 6. 'by a person duly licensed to drive it'

This means that if anyone is in attendance at the vehicle, to escape committing an offence under this regulation he or she must be the holder of a current driving licence for that class of vehicle.

■ 7. 'without the engine being stopped'

This point means that, apart from the exceptions at regulation 107(2)(a) and (b) (the main ones are shown at point 4 above), the engines of all motor vehicles must be stopped when the vehicles are unattended.

■ 8. 'without the parking brake being effectively set'.

Means that the handbrake (in the case of a saloon motor car) was not set. The driver could have applied the brake but because of a defective ratchet, for instance, the brake could have slipped and as a result would not be effectively set.

(C) USUAL METHODS OF PROVING THESE POINTS

■ 1. 'That you' See (C)1 of offence 1.

■ 2. 'did cause (or permit)'

See (C)2 of offence 5.

■ 3. 'to be on a road called ....'

See (C)4 of offence 1.

■ 4. 'a motor vehicle, namely a ....'

See (C)3 of offence 1.

■ 5. 'which was not attended'

Generally this point is proved by the officer finding an unattended vehicle with the engine running. After making unsuccessful inquiries to find the driver in the immediate area, these facts can be used to prove the unattended element.

■ 6. 'by a person duly licensed to drive it'

The problem of 'hearsay evidence' can occur where a passenger in a motor vehicle has to be asked whether or not he holds a current licence for the class of vehicle.

A way round this hearsay evidence is for the officer to say, for example: 'The passenger Mr Jones says he is not licensed to drive this car so I am reporting you (the defendant) for quitting a vehicle' etc.

If the passenger is not in possession of a licence, but states he is the holder of the necessary licence, further inquiries will be made by the police officer to ascertain whether or not he is a duly licensed driver. If not, the defendant driver can be seen later and told he will be reported.

■ 7. 'without the engine being stopped'

This point can be proved by the observations of the officer dealing, namely, 'The engine was running, ignition key switched on, exhaust fumes coming from exhaust pipe' etc.

■ 8. 'without the parking brake being effectively set'.

This point can be proved by pushing the vehicle along the road to show there was no braking effect; by things speaking for themselves where the unattended vehicle runs away down hill; and by observing the handbrake lever in the off position etc.

Failing to set the handbrake is sometimes detected when it is too late, ie when a vehicle has been parked unattended and has then begun to move and run away downhill, perhaps resulting in an accident. In such a case a careful examination of the handbrake should be made bearing this offence in mind.

If necessary the prosecution might call a vehicle examiner to give evidence where there is some technical failure of the handbrake such as a worn ratchet causing the brake lever to slip or a frayed cable which snapped under pressure.

(D) SUPPORTING EVIDENCE

Note. A person failing to set the handbrake can also be reported for leaving a vehicle in a dangerous position contrary to section 22 Road Traffic Act 1988.

25. HORNS NOT FITTED
Regulation 37 Road Vehicles (Construction and Use) Regs 1986 and section 42 Road Traffic Act 1988

(A) POINTS TO PROVE
1. That you 2. did use (or cause or permit to be used) 3. on a road called .... 4. a motor vehicle namely a .... 5. which was not fitted 6. with an instrument capable of giving audible and sufficient warning of its approach or position.

(B) MEANING OF TERMS
■ **1. 'That you'**
This point means the identity of the person using, causing or permitting to be used.
■ **2. 'did use (or cause or permit to be used)'**
See Glossary.
■ **3. 'on a road called ....'**
See Glossary.
■ **4. 'a motor vehicle namely a ....'**
See Glossary. The vehicle must have a maximum speed of more than 20mph.
■ **5. 'which was not fitted'**
This point means that either the motor vehicle in question had no horn fitted at all or that the one that was fitted did not conform to the requirements of the next point.
■ **6. 'with an instrument capable of giving audible and sufficient warning of its approach or position'.**
This point means that the horn if not fitted would hardly be able to warn people. If fitted it has got to work sufficiently well to warn other road users of its approach etc. Therefore horns with loose wires where the sound emitted is not continuous and reliable or where the sound is too soft, etc would not comply with this regulation.

(C) USUAL METHODS OF PROVING THESE POINTS

■ 1. 'That you'
See (C)1 of offence 1.

■ 2. 'did use (or cause or permit to be used)'
See (C)2 of offence 5, and in the case of 'use' for construction and use offences see (C)2 of offence 19.

■ 3. 'on a road called ....'
See (C)4 of offence number 1.

■ 4. 'a motor vehicle namely a ....'
See (C)3 of offence number 1.

■ 5. 'which was not fitted'
This point is proved by an examination of the motor vehicle, which in these days of mass produced cars will generally reveal that a horn is fitted. In a few cases where a horn has been removed this can be proved by stating so or by an admission on the part of the defendant. In most cases the horn will be fitted and although it is not necessary to prove why the horn didn't work when operated it may be of assistance to the court.

In practice it is better to show in evidence for the prosecution that the defendant was also asked to try to get the horn to work as explained at point (D)(b) of offence 20.

■ 6. 'with an instrument capable of giving audible and sufficient warning of its approach or position'
This point is proved simply by no sound or insufficient sound being emitted when the horn, if any, is tested. Common sense will have to prevail as to whether the noise emitted is sufficient or not.

(D) SUPPORTING EVIDENCE

Note. Several points of interest relating to horns are dealt with at other parts of regulation 37 as below.

(4) Subject to paragraphs (5) (6) and (7) no motor vehicle shall be fitted with a gong, bell, siren or two-tone horn.

(5) The following vehicles may be fitted with a gong, bell, siren or two-tone horn:

(a) motor vehicles used for fire brigade, ambulance or police purposes;

(b) motor vehicles owned by a body formed primarily for the purpose of fire salvage and used for those or similar purposes;

(c) motor vehicles owned by the Forestry Commission or by local authorities and used from time to time for the purpose of fighting fires;

(d) motor vehicles owned by the Secretary of State for Defence and used for the purposes of the disposal of bombs or explosives;

(e) motor vehicles used for the purposes of the Blood Transfusion Service provided under the National Health Service Act 1977 or under the National Health Service (Scotland) Act 1947;

(f) motor vehicles used by Her Majesty's Coastguard or the Coastguard Auxiliary Service to aid persons in danger or vessels in distress on or near the coast;

(g) motor vehicles owned by the [National Coal Board] and used for the purposes of rescue operations at mines;

(h) motor vehicles owned by the Secretary of State for Defence and used by the Royal Air Force Mountain Rescue Service for the purposes of rescue operations in connection with crashed aircraft or any other emergencies; and

(i) motor vehicles owned by the Royal National Lifeboat Institution and used for the purposes of launching lifeboats.

(6) The provisions of paragraphs (2) and (4) above shall not apply so as to make it unlawful for a motor vehicle to be fitted with an instrument or apparatus other than a two-tone horn designed to emit a sound for the purpose of informing members of the public that goods are on the vehicle for sale. Colonel Bogey type horns and other such ditties are now unlawful on vehicles first used on or after August 1, 1973.

Further paragraphs deal with bells, gongs or sirens being used for theft prevention purposes or to summons help for the conductors, drivers and inspectors of large passenger-carrying vehicles. Regulation 37(2) requires that the sound emitted by any horn (other than a reversing alarm or two-tone horn) fitted to a wheeled vehicle first used on or after 1 August 1973, shall be continuous and uniform and not strident.

26. PEDESTRIAN FAILING TO COMPLY WITH CONSTABLE'S DIRECTION
Section 37 Road Traffic Act 1988

(A) POINTS TO PROVE
1. That you 2. being a person on foot 3. where a police constable (or a traffic warden) in uniform 4. was engaged in the regulation of vehicular traffic in a road 5. did proceed across (or along) the carriageway 6. in contravention of a direction to stop given by the constable (or the traffic warden) in the execution of his duty.

(B) MEANING OF TERMS
■ **1. 'That you'**
Means the identity of the pedestrian. Under section 169 of this Act a constable may require a person committing an offence under section 37 to give his name and address, and if that person fails to do so he is guilty of an offence.
■ **2. 'being a person on foot'**
Means walking or running etc as opposed to being carried in or on a vehicle or riding a horse etc. It has been held that a person on foot pushing a bicycle when using a zebra pedestrian crossing was a 'foot passenger'.
■ **3. 'where a police constable (or a traffic warden) in uniform'**

Means a police constable (as opposed to a cadet) or a traffic warden, both of whom must be in uniform. It has been held under the drink/driving law that the object of requiring the officer to be 'in uniform' was to ensure that the constable would be easily recognised as such by the public.

■ **4. 'was engaged in the regulation of vehicular traffic in a road'**

See (B)4 of offence 12. See Glossary for 'road'.

■ **5. 'did proceed across (or along) the carriageway'**

This point means that the pedestrian tried or succeeded in walking across the carriageway, ie from footpath to footpath or along the carriageway in the same direction as the traffic flow.

■ **6. 'in contravention of a direction to stop given by the constable (or the traffic warden) in the execution of his duty'.**

The signal must be given clearly. See (B)7 of offence 12. 'Execution of his duty' means that he should be acting in the protection of life and property.

(C) USUAL METHODS OF PROVING THESE POINTS

■ **1. 'That you'**

See (C)1 of offence 1.

■ **2. 'being a person on foot'**

This point is proved by the officer or traffic warden stating in evidence, 'A man, I now know to be John Smith, stepped from the kerb on the south side of the road and walked towards me in contravention of my signal to him to stop etc'.

■ **3. 'where a police constable (or a traffic warden) in uniform'**

This point can be proved by starting the officer's or the warden's evidence by, 'I am a police constable (or traffic warden) in such and such a police force and I was in uniform'. Usually nothing further need be proved in relation to uniform but where problems can be envisaged because an officer had no helmet or tunic on, then the general appearance of the officer could be put in evidence if required in the case of a 'not guilty' plea.

■ 4. 'was engaged in the regulation of vehicular traffic'

This point is proved by the officer or warden stating in evidence that, 'I was engaged in the regulation of traffic to allow pedestrians to cross safely etc'.

■ 5. 'did proceed across (or along) the carriageway'

This point is proved by the officer or warden describing what the defendant did to contravene the signal as at point 2 above.

■ 6. 'in contravention of a direction to stop given by the constable (or the traffic warden) in the execution of his duty'.

The officer or warden should describe how he gave the necessary signal, eg, 'I raised my right arm with the palm of my hand facing the defendant. The signal was clearly visible etc ....'. The execution of duty is proved as at 4 above.

27. PARKING ON WRONG SIDE AT NIGHT

Regulation 101 Road Vehicles (Construction and Use) Regulations 1986 and section 42 Road Traffic Act 1988

(A) POINTS TO PROVE

1. That you 2. did cause (or permit) 3. a motor vehicle, namely a .... 4. to stand on a road called ....
5. between the hours of sunset and sunrise 6. otherwise than with the left or nearside of the vehicle as close as may be to the edge of the carriageway.

(B) MEANING OF TERMS

■ 1. 'That you'

Means the identity of the person causing or permitting the offence.

■ **2. 'did cause (or permit)'**
Note that 'using' is not included.
■ **3. 'a motor vehicle, namely a ....**
See Glossary.
■ **4. 'to stand on a road called ....**
'Stand' means, in general parlance, parked.
■ **5. 'between the hours of sunset and sunrise'**
Sunset and sunrise are to be taken at the place where the alleged
offences were committed.
■ **6. 'otherwise than with the left or nearside of the vehicle
as close as may be to the edge of the carriageway'.**
This phrase means what it says. Obviously a line has to be
drawn somewhere. Should a driver be prosecuted for being
10cm away from the kerb, or a metre away from the kerb?
The circumstances of each case must be the deciding factor as
the narrower the road the more important this offence
becomes.

(C) USUAL METHODS OF PROVING THESE POINTS
■ **1. 'That you'**
See (C)1 of offence 1.
■ **2. 'did cause (or permit)'**
See (C)2 of offence 5.
■ **3. 'a motor vehicle, namely a ....'**
See (C)3 of offence 1.
■ **4. 'to stand on a road called ....'**
See (C)4 of offence 1 for 'road'.
'Stand' is proved by the observations of the officer concerned
and although it is not necessary to prove that the vehicle had
been in the offending position for a particular period of time the
court may find it helpful if the officer could give evidence of it,
'The vehicle was parked on Bradford Road from 20.00 hours to
21.00 hours etc'.
■ **5. 'between the hours of sunset and sunrise'**

This point is proved in accordance with local custom if it is found necessary. Some courts accept the officer's word and some refer to almanacs etc.

■ **6. 'otherwise than with the left or nearside of the vehicle as close as may be to the edge of the carriageway'.**

This point is proved by showing in evidence that the vehicle was the wrong way round, ie the offside or right of the vehicle was next to the kerb or that the nearside was not as close as may be to the kerb.

(D) SUPPORTING EVIDENCE

Note 1. The exceptions to this offence are:

(a) any motor vehicle when it is being used for fire brigade, ambulance or police purposes or for defence purposes (including civil defence purposes) if compliance with this regulation would hinder or be likely to hinder the use of the vehicle for the purpose for which it is being used on that occasion;

(b) any motor vehicle standing on a part of a road specially set aside for the parking of vehicles, or as a stand for hackney carriages, or as a stand for public service vehicles, or as a place at which such vehicles may stop for a longer time than is necessary for the taking up and setting down of passengers where compliance with this regulation would conflict with the provisions of any order, regulations or bylaws governing the use of such part of a road for that purpose;

(c) any motor vehicle waiting to set down or pick up passengers in accordance with regulations made or directions given by the chief officer of police in regard to such setting down or picking up;

(d) any motor vehicle on any road in which vehicles are allowed to proceed in one direction only; or

(e) any motor vehicle while it is being used in connection with -

   (i)   any building operation or demolition;

   (ii) the repair of any other vehicle;

   (iii) the removal of any obstruction to traffic;

   (iv) the maintenance, repair or reconstruction of any road; or

   (v) the laying, erection, alteration or repair in or near to any road of any sewer, or any main, pipe or apparatus for the supply of gas, water or electricity, of any telegraph or telephone wires, cables, posts or supports or of the apparatus of any electric transport undertaking if, in any such case, compliance with this regulation would hinder or be likely to hinder the use of the vehicle for the purpose for which it is being used on that occasion.

28. FAIL TO CONFORM TO PELICAN/PUFFIN LIGHTS

Regulation 23, Zebra, Pelican and Puffin Pedestrian Crossing Regulations 1997 and section 25 Road Traffic Regulation Act 1984

(A) POINTS TO PROVE

1. That you 2. being the driver/rider of a vehicle, namely a .... 3. did fail to comply 4. with a vehicular light signal 5. at a Pelican/Puffin crossing on .... (give location) 6. which was displaying a red light.

(B) MEANING OF TERMS

■ 1. 'That you'

Means the identity of the person driving.

■ 2. 'being the driver/rider of a vehicle, namely a .... '

See Glossary for 'driver'. 'Rider' includes motor bikes and pedal cycles. The make and registration number of motor vehicles should be shown.

■ **3. 'did fail to comply'**

Means did not stop at the 'stop line'. The stop line is a solid white line across the carriageway between 1.7 and three metres (four-and-a-half to 10 feet) before the first line of studs indicating the start of the crossing (the part where the pedestrians walk).

■ **4. 'with a vehicular light signal'**

Means the red light of the light sequence.

■ **5. 'at a Pelican/Puffin crossing on ....'**

'Pelican' crossings look like a set of traffic lights with a similar light sequence - except that after the red 'stop' signal, a flashing amber light allows traffic to proceed if the crossing is clear. The crossing lights are controlled by a pedestrian-operated button.

'Puffin' crossing are similar to a set of traffic lights and the light sequence is the same. They use sensors to detect anyone waiting to cross or actually crossing and keep the lights at red until crossing is complete.

The location of the crossing should be shown.

■ **6. 'which was displaying a red light'.**

The red light is mandatory and means that vehicles must stop at the 'stop line'.

(C) USUAL METHODS OF PROVING THESE POINTS

■ **1. 'That you'**

See (C)1 of offence 1.

■ **2. 'being the driver/rider of a vehicle, namely a ....'**

See (C)2 and (C)3 of offence 1 for 'driver' and 'mechanically propelled vehicle'. Riding vehicles would be proved by witness(es) or on the admission of the rider.

■ **3. 'did cause the vehicle (or part of the vehicle)'**

Proved by witness(es)' statements showing that the vehicle did not stop at the stop line.

■ **4. 'with a vehicular light signal'**

Again, a witness, usually a police officer, would say the signal was showing a red light as the vehicle went over the stop line.

■ 5 'at a Pelican/Puffin crossing on ....'.

The particular crossing contravened must be described accurately in a witness statement, together with its location. For example: 'I was observing the Pelican button-operated crossing on New Street outside the Town Hall entrance....'

■ 6. 'which was displaying a red light'.

As as point 4 above.

(D) SUPPORTING EVIDENCE

Note 1. This offence does not require a notice of intended prosecution to be served on the driver. According to regulation 12(2) and 13(2) of these Regulations, a driver has the overall responsibility to proceed with due regard to the safety of other users of the road (subject to the direction of any police constable or traffic warden).

Note 2. Be aware of other offences associated with crossings such as:

    (a) loitering on a crossing - which may apply to children 'playing' with the buttons or sensors;

    (b) stopping within controlled areas;

    (c) overtaking on the approach to a crossing.

29. DEFECTIVE SIDE LIGHTS (COMMITTED ANY TIME)

Regulation 23(1) Road Vehicles Lighting Regulations 1989 and section 42(1) Road Traffic Act 1988

(A) POINTS TO PROVE

1. That you 2. did use (or cause, or permit to be used) 3. on a road called .... 4. a certain motor vehicle namely a .... 5. the lighting equipment of which required by

these Regulations to be fitted, namely .... (here specify)
6. was not clean and in good working order 7. in
contravention of a statutory provision relating to
obligatory lamps (or reflectors) and applicable to that
vehicle, namely ....

(B) MEANING OF TERMS

■ 1. 'That you'
Means the identity of the person using the motor vehicle etc.

■ 2. 'did use (or cause or permit to be used)'
This offence can also be committed when the vehicle is stationary.

■ 3. 'on a road called ....'
See Glossary.

■ 4. 'a certain motor vehicle, namely a ....'
See Glossary.

■ 5. 'the lighting equipment of which required by these Regulations to be fitted, namely .... (here specify)'
This point means that all the statutory provisions regarding obligatory lamps and reflectors, before the vehicle can lawfully be driven, must be complied with. The most common statutory provisions require two white lights to the front and two red lights and two reflectors to the rear.

■ 6. 'was not clean and in good working order'
This point means among other things that the lamps in question must be kept clean as mud or snow could hide the light. The bulb must be in good working order and the wiring must be good, ie free from any short circuits or bad earths which could adversely affect the lamp.

■ 7. 'in contravention of a statutory provision relating to obligatory lamps (or reflectors) and applicable to that vehicle, namely ....'
Examples of common contraventions of statutory provisions are shown at point 6 above.

(C) USUAL METHODS OF PROVING THESE POINTS
■ 1. 'That you'
See (C)1 of offence 1.
■ 2. 'did use (or cause or permit to be used)'
See (C)2 of offence 5. For further information regarding proving 'use' in relation to construction and use offences, see (C)2 of offence 19.
■ 3. 'on a road called ....'
See (C)4 of offence 1.
■ 4. 'a certain motor vehicle, namely a ....'
See (C)3 of offence 1.
■ 5. 'the lighting equipment of which required by these Regulations to be fitted, namely .... (here specify)'
This point is proved by showing whatever is specified is the lamp or reflector in question, eg, the obligatory front nearside lamp or the rear offside reflector etc.
■ 6. 'was not clean and in good working order'
The defect must be described in detail to prove this point, eg, 'Both bulbs were blown in the front obligatory lights and two white lights were not being shown to the front' or, 'The rear nearside reflector was broken and part of it was missing, leaving only about a square centimetre of reflective material' etc.
■ 7. 'in contravention of a statutory provision relating to obligatory lamps (or reflectors) and applicable to that vehicle, namely ....'
As this offence can be committed at any time the fact that it was dark at the time could be shown to assist the court in deciding on punishment.

(D) SUPPORTING EVIDENCE
The times of sunset and sunrise can be proved by reference to an almanac. Where the time is crucial to the offence the prosecution should be in a position to be able to prove the actual times in that locality from observations, should they be so required.

Note 1. This offence does not apply to –
(a) a rear fog lamp on a vehicle which is part of a combination of vehicles any part of which is not required by the Regulations to be fitted with a rear fog lamp;
(b) a rear fog lamp on a motor vehicle drawing a trailer; or
(c) a lamp, reflector or rear marking which, during daytime hours is fitted to a combat vehicle.
 A 'combat vehicle' is a military vehicle used for the carriage of tanks, guns etc.
Note 2. An offence will not be committed when a defective lamp or reflector is found on a vehicle in use on a road between sunrise and sunset if such a lamp or reflector became defective during the journey which is in progress or if arrangements have been made to remedy the defect with all reasonable expedition.

30. INTERFERENCE WITH VEHICLES
Section 9 Criminal Attempts Act 1981

(A) POINTS TO PROVE
1. That you 2. did interfere 3. with a motor vehicle (or trailer) (or with anything carried in or on a motor vehicle or trailer) 4. with the intention that a specified offence shall be committed by yourself or another.

(B) MEANING OF TERMS
■ **1. 'That you'**
This means the person interfering with a motor vehicle etc.
■ **2. 'did interfere'**
The dictionary definition of 'interfere' is to meddle with or come into collision with something. Therefore any meddling with a vehicle with intent to steal it or part of it etc would amount to 'interference'. Examples would include prising the hub caps off, breaking a door lock, trying to remove badges or

mascots, twisting electric wires together, breaking a steering lock, etc.

The essence of this offence is to protect the vehicle before an actual theft or 'taking without the owner's consent' takes place.

■ **3. 'with a motor vehicle (or trailer) (or with anything carried in or on a motor vehicle or trailer)'**

'Motor vehicle' and 'trailer' have the same meanings assigned to them as under the Road Traffic Act 1988, see Glossary.

'Anything carried in or on a motor vehicle or trailer' includes the roof rack or its contents; articles inside a vehicle such as maps, coats, bags etc; goods in vans or lorries or trailers etc.

■ **4. 'with the intention that a specified offence shall be committed by yourself or another.'**

The mental element of this offence is that the 'interference' must be, in the accused's mind, for the purpose of committing a specified offence by himself or by another.

The specified offences are:

   (a)   theft of the motor vehicle or trailer, or part of it;

   (b)   theft of anything carried in or on the motor vehicle or trailer; and

   (c)   section 12(1) Theft Act 1968 (take and drive away without consent).

Note that if it is shown that the accused intended that any one of these offences should be committed, it matters not that it cannot be shown which it was.

(C) USUAL METHODS OF PROVING THESE POINTS
■ **1. 'That you'**

In these days of videoed car parks, the video may help to prove the identity of the offender. Otherwise witness statements and/or the interview would be the most likely way.

■ **2. 'did interfere'**

Again video evidence or the statement of a witness would provide the proof of this point. For example: 'I saw the youth smash the quarter light glass of the rear offside passenger door and put his hand through…'

■ **3. 'with a motor vehicle (or trailer) (or with anything carried in or on a motor vehicle or trailer)'**

This point is normally proved by describing the make, model etc of the motor vehicle or trailer, in the police officer's or other witness statement. If the interference is with something carried in or on the motor vehicle or trailer the witness statement may read, 'I saw the man untie the straps of the trailer tarpaulin at the read of the trailer and lift up the tarpaulin. . .'

■ **4. 'with the intention that a specified offence shall be committed, by yourself or another'.**

A person's 'intent' can be proved in a variety of ways. For example, either by his own admission; by the facts speaking for themselves (r*es ipsa loquitur*); by him telling a witness of his intentions before embarking on the crime; or by other circumstantial evidence such as the accused needing spare parts for his 'hot hatch' and the one he is interfering with happens to be the same model and colour etc.

The best and strongest evidence would be admissions during the interview that the accused intended, for example, to steal the car to break it up for parts; to take it without consent for a joy ride; or to steal the mobile phone and sheepskin jacket lying on the back seat. If the accused did not intend to commit a specified offence himself but was interfering with the motor vehicle to enable a more 'skilled' person to 'hot wire' the car, then this would be proved in their respective interviews.

(D) SUPPORTING EVIDENCE

Note 1. As already mentioned, this offence of 'interfering' is normally used where the more serious offences are not completed, ie, the actual theft of the car or its parts or its load etc. The offence can be committed anywhere.

Note 2. Other connected offences include:

(a) 'tampering with a motor vehicle' but this offence is restricted to a road or local authority parking place where the person gets on the vehicle or tampers with the brake or other part of its mechanism (section 25 Road Traffic Act 1988);

(b) 'going equipped for stealing' (section 25 Theft Act 1968) see offence 18 - taking a conveyance is included in 'theft'; and

(c) 'taking a conveyance without the owners' consent, or knowing it has been so taken, or drives or allows himself/herself to be carried in or on it' (section 12(1) Theft Act 1968) see offence 11.

Section 2

Crime

1. WASTING POLICE TIME
Section 5 (2) Criminal Law Act 1967

(A) POINTS TO PROVE
1. That you 2. did cause wasteful employment of the police 3. by knowingly making a false report to ....
(specify person, not necessarily a constable) 4. (a) tending to show that an offence had been committed; or (b) to give rise to apprehension for the safety of any person (or property); (c) to show that you had information material to a police inquiry.

(B) MEANING OF TERMS
■ **1. 'That you'**
Means the identity of the person committing the offence.
■ **2. 'did cause wasteful employment of the police'**
Means that the offender actually caused police time to be wasted in one of the three ways listed at point 4, ie falsely reporting a possible offence, danger to a person(s) or property or that the reporter had material information.
■ **3. 'by knowingly making a false report to ....'**
This point shows that guilty knowledge must be present. The offence is not 'making a false report', but 'knowingly making a false report'. The person to whom the report was made should also be named to help to establish guilt.
■ **4. (a) 'tending to show that an offence had been committed, or'**
This point includes conduct such as a straightforward report of a false crime to anyone, but it will usually be made to a constable, eg that a person's car has been stolen or taken without authority or that a house has been burgled.
■ **4. (b) 'to give rise to apprehension for the safety of any person (or property) or'**
False reports that a person is missing from home or that a bomb

is in a building (which is more likely to be encountered in practice) come under this point. Note the offence of making a bomb hoax call etc, under section 51(2) Criminal Law Act 1977. There is no requirement for the Director of Public Prosecutions' consent for section 51.

■ **4. (c) 'to show that you had information material to a police inquiry'.**

This point includes a person who falsely reports that he knows who is responsible for a particular crime or where stolen property etc, is hidden. It is difficult to pinpoint any one category of persons likely to commit this offence as a variety of motives will be involved.

(C) USUAL METHODS OF PROVING THESE POINTS
■ **1. 'That you'**

The identity of the offender can be proved by the person who took the false report stating who he took it from. Problems might arise when the false report is made via a telephone. In such cases the witness can try to identify the voice, but the best evidence is an admission by the offender that he was the caller.

■ **2. 'did cause wasteful employment of the police'**

The police should be in a position to prove how many hours are actually wasted. The hours can be calculated by totalling all the man hours expended as a result of the false report, eg a false report is made by a driver, involved in a hit and run accident, that his car had been stolen and at the time of the accident it must have been driven by the thief and not himself. If two constables spent ten hours each investigating the false report before discovering the truth then the total hours wasted would be 20.

■ **3. 'by knowingly making a false report to ....
(Specify person, not necessarily a constable)'**

This point has to be proved and in common with other offences where 'what a person knows' has to be proved, difficulties can arise. A judge has said that the state of a man's mind is as much a fact as the state of his digestion. But unless the defendant admits he knew the report to be false the prosecution will have to rely on circumstantial evidence. The easiest way to prove this point is to ask a question like 'Did you know the report you made to .... (person's name) was false?' and if the answer is 'Yes' then this would be good evidence.

Circumstantial evidence could take the form of showing the defendant wished to cover up an offence committed by himself, such as driving over the prescribed limit, being involved in an accident and then, as mentioned at (C) 2 ante, alleging that someone else was driving at the time of the accident. The report need not be made to a constable. A false report of theft could be made to a next-door neighbour, perhaps to cover up for dealing with property wrongfully, and then the neighbour could make a genuine report to the police about the false theft, thereby causing police time to be wasted. The neighbour would not be liable for this offence, but the person who made the false report could probably be prosecuted.

■ **4. (a) 'tending to show that an offence had been committed, or'**

This point can be proved by what was said in the report. The person, who took the report should include the exact words or writing of the report in his evidence and show that the report tended towards showing that an offence had been committed.

■ **4. (b) and (c).**

These points can be proved as in point 4(a) above, with the end result being suitably altered.

(D) SUPPORTING EVIDENCE

This offence cannot be proceeded with except by or with the consent of the Director of Public Prosecutions. Such consent helps to provide uniformity among police forces when considering prosecuting for an offence which can be committed in so many different ways and for so many different reasons.

2A. FEAR OR PROVOCATION OF VIOLENCE
Section 4(1) Public Order Act 1986

(See Racial Aggravation Chart at offence 2E.)

(A) POINTS TO PROVE
1. That you 2. did at .... 3. use towards another person 4. threatening or abusive or insulting words or behaviour or distribute or display to another person any writing, sign or other visible representation, namely ...., which is threatening abusive or insulting, 5. with intent to cause that person to believe that immediate unlawful violence would be used against him or another by a person, or 6. to provoke the immediate use of unlawful violence by that person or another or 7. whereby that person is likely to believe that such violence would be used or it is likely that such violence would be provoked.

(B) MEANING OF TERMS
■ 1. 'That you'
Means the identity of the offender.
■ 2. 'did at ....'
The place where the offence was committed should be inserted here. Section 4(2) of the Public Order Act 1986 extends the old section 5 breach of the peace offence by providing: 'An offence under this section may be committed in a public or a private place, except that no offence is committed where the words or behaviour are used, or the writing, sign or other visible representation is distributed or displayed, by a person inside a dwelling and the other person is also inside that or another dwelling'. 'Dwelling' means any structure or part of a structure occupied as a person's home or as other living accommodation (whether the occupation is separate or shared with others) but does not include any part not so occupied, and for this purpose 'structure'

includes a tent, caravan, vehicle, vessel or other temporary or movable structure (section 8).

■ **3. 'use towards another person'**

This phrase means that the threats etc, must be towards another person. In other words, no offence would be committed if another(s) was (or were) not present who could be abused, insulted or threatened etc. In *Atkin v DPP* (1989) 153 JP 383 it was held that the words 'uses towards another person' mean that threatening words must be addressed directly to another person who is present and either in earshot or aimed at as being putatively in earshot.

It is inappropriate to use the words 'another person' in an information charging an offence under section 4 Public Order Act 1986 because the person having the belief that unlawful violence would be used has to be the SAME PERSON as the person threatened, abused or insulted, *Loade v DPP* (1990) 90 Cr App R 162.

■ **4. 'threatening or abusive or insulting words or behaviour or distribute or display to another person any writing, sign or other visible representation, namely .... which is threatening, abusive or insulting'**

The phrases mean the same as under the old section 5 Public Order Act 1936.

Threatening, abusive or insulting should be given their ordinary meanings. Words or behaviour show that the offence can be committed by using words or merely by actions or behaviour. Distributes or displays to another person any writing, sign or other visible representation, should all be given their ordinary meanings. This means the giving out or showing of any written matter or a sign, eg sandwich board, or other visible representation which would threaten, abuse or insult another person. In practice it is more common to find the words or behaviour part of the offence being breached rather than the distributing or displaying part.

The whole phrase under this point only creates one offence and section 7(2) of the 1986 Act provides that for the purposes of the rules against charging more than one offence in the same count or information, each of sections 1 to 5 create one offence. Therefore, it would be correct to charge 'using threatening and insulting words and behaviour ....'.

The mental element or *mens rea* of the offender for this point is as follows: section 6(3) provides that a person is guilty of an offence under section 4 only if he intends his words or behaviour, or the writing, sign or other visible representation, to be threatening, abusive or insulting, or is aware that it may be threatening, abusive or insulting.

This means that the offender's words, behaviour, writing, sign or visible representation must be deliberately threatening, abusive or insulting as opposed to reckless, accidental or blamelessly inadvertent.

If such intent cannot be shown, the awareness part of this mental element definition could be used. This is easier to prove and would require the subjective examination of the offender by asking questions such as, 'Would an offender of the level of his intelligence have been aware?'

■ 5. 'with intent to cause that person to believe that immediate unlawful violence would be used against him or another by any person'

This means a deliberate frame of mind on the part of the offender to cause a certain belief on the part of the victim. This is a hard part to prove and where the evidence of intent falls short, the point at 7 following, ie, 'whereby that person is likely to believe ....' could be charged or reported.

Whether the victim did believe that immediate violence would be used is immaterial so long as the offender intended to cause the victim to have that belief.

Immediate unlawful violence means that circumstances involving delayed violence or lawful violence, such as a lawful rugby tackle during a game, would not amount to this offence.

'Violence' means any violent conduct, so that:

(a) except in the context of affray, it includes violent conduct towards property as well as violent conduct towards persons, and

(b) it is not restricted to conduct causing or intended to cause injury or damage but includes any other violent conduct (for example, throwing at or towards a person a missile of a kind capable of causing injury which does not hit or falls short) (section 8).

'Would be used against him or another by any person' means against the victim or the victim's baby, friend or spouse etc, The offender need not be the person to offer the violence as a friend of the offender would come within the phrase, 'by any person'.

■ 6. 'to provoke the immediate use of unlawful violence by that person or another'

The intent to provoke the immediate use of unlawful violence means an intention by the offender to cause the other party or another to use unlawful violence.

■ 7. 'whereby that person is likely to believe that such violence would be used or it is likely that such violence would be provoked'.

This is the easier part of the offence to prove. In the first instance where the police officer dealing with the offender cannot prove an intent, as point 5 above, he should consider this point. 'Likely to believe' or 'likely to be provoked' means, that in the opinion of the police officer and the court, these likelihoods might occur. Note that for this part of the offence to be proved neither likelihood need occur. It was held in *R v Horseferry Road Metropolitan Stipendiary Magistrate, ex p Siadatan* [1991] 1 All ER 324 that the phrase 'such violence' must be 'immediate' and the phrase refers back to the words 'immediate unlawful violence.'

(C) USUAL METHODS OF PROVING THESE POINTS

■ 1. 'That you'.

This point is proved by the officer who arrests the suspect stating that the defendant in court is the person involved. Any witness could prove this point.

■ 2. 'did at ....'

The location of the offence can be described in evidence by any witness of the incident to show that it occurred in a public or a private place. Note the offence cannot be committed inside a dwelling when the other person is inside that or another dwelling.

■ 3. 'use towards another person'

This can be proved by a civilian witness or a police officer witnessing the incident and describing in his evidence that the threats etc, were towards the other person. There is no requirement to identify the other person but this may be advantageous in certain circumstances, eg when it is suspected that a defence may be used that there was no other person.

■ 4. 'threatening or abusive or insulting words or behaviour or distribute or display to another person any writing, sign or other visible representation, namely .... which is threatening, abusive or insulting'

The type of actions used by the offender should be explained in the witness statement(s). The actual words (if any) should be recorded, eg, 'You bastard, I'll cripple you here and now'. The mental element or mens rea under section 6(3) should be considered at this point. Good questioning is essential to prove clearly an intent or awareness on the part of the offender. For example: 'Did you intend to threaten, abuse and insult that person when you said, "You bastard, I'll cripple you here and now"? He replied, "No". I said, "Were you aware that you might threaten, abuse or insult him?" He said, "Yes".'

■ 5. 'with intent to cause that person to believe that immediate unlawful violence would be used against him or another by any person'

This point, if used, can be proved by the officer in the case questioning the offender, eg, 'Did you want that Notown Football Club supporter to believe that you and your friends were going to hit him?' He said, "Yes, but I wasn't going to hit him".'

■ 6. 'to provoke the immediate use of unlawful violence by that person or another'

If this point is charged or reported it may be proved by the officer in the case questioning the offender on the lines of: 'Did you intend to provoke the Notown football supporters into violence? He said, "Yes, I wanted you lads to catch them at it and arrest them".'

■ 7. 'whereby that person is likely to believe that such violence would be used or it is likely that such violence would be provoked'.

The officer dealing and/or civilian witnesses could help prove this point by including in their evidence observations, such as:

'The crowd of visiting football supporters were likely to believe they were going to be attacked', or, 'It was likely that the visiting supporters would lose their tempers and attack the home crowd'.

(D) SUPPORTING EVIDENCE

Note 1. It was held under the Public Order Act 1936 that a police officer could be the 'other' person.

Note 2. In *Winn v DPP* (1992) 156 JP 881 it was held that although section 4 creates only one offence, that offence may be committed in four different ways. Common to all four is the requirement that the accused must intend or be aware that his words or behaviour are or may be threatening, abusive or insulting and must be directed to another person.

Note 3. Note that the additional offence under section 31 of the Crime and Disorder Act 1998 is also committed if 'racially aggravated' (see Racial Aggravation Chart at offence 2E)

2B. CONDUCT LIKELY TO CAUSE HARASSMENT, ALARM OR DISTRESS
Section 5 Public Order Act 1986

(See Racial Aggravation Chart at offence 2E.)

(A) POINTS TO PROVE
1. That you 2. did at .... 3. use threatening, abusive or insulting words or behaviour, 4. or disorderly behaviour, or 5. display any writing, sign or other visible representation which was threatening, abusive or insulting, 6. within the hearing or sight of a person 7. likely to be caused harassment, alarm or distress.

(B) MEANING OF TERMS
■ 1. 'That you,'
Means the identity of the disorderly person.
■ 2. 'did at ....'
This point means that under section 5(2) and (3) an offence under this section may be committed in a public or private place, except that no offence is committed where the words or behaviour are used, or the writing, sign or other visible representation is displayed by a person inside a dwelling and the other person is also inside that or another dwelling.

It is a defence for the accused to prove:
(a) that he had no reason to believe that there was any person within hearing or sight who was likely to be caused harassment, alarm or distress; or
(b) that he was inside a dwelling and had no reason to believe that the words or behaviour used, or the writing, sign or other visible representation displayed, would be heard or seen by a person outside that or any other dwelling; or
(c) that his conduct was reasonable.

Note that 'dwelling' means any structure or part of a structure occupied as a person's home or as other living accommodation (whether the occupation is separate or shared with others) but does not include any part not so occupied, and for this purpose 'structure' includes a tent, caravan, vehicle, vessel or other temporary or movable structure.

■ **3. 'use threatening, abusive or insulting words or behaviour'**
Threatening, abusive or insulting should be given their ordinary meanings. Words or behaviour show that the offence can be committed by using words or merely by actions or behaviour. The whole phrase does not create more than one offence.

Under section 7(2) - for the purposes of the rules against charging more than one offence in the same count or information - each of sections 1 to 5 creates one offence.

The state of mind or *mens rea* required for this offence is explained in section 6(4) viz: A person is guilty of an offence under section 5 only if he intends his words or behaviour, or the writing, sign or other visible representation, to be threatening, abusive or insulting, or is aware that it may be threatening, abusive or insulting; or (as the case may be) he intends his behaviour to be or is aware that it may be disorderly.

Only those points (B)3, 4 and 5 of this offence are reflected in section 6(4) as per *DPP v Clarke* [1992] Crim LR 60

■ **4. 'or disorderly behaviour'**
This point is not defined but it is felt that any conduct which is not orderly and is not covered by 'threatening, abusive, or insulting words or behaviour' would suffice.

Note the defence if the accused can prove that his conduct was reasonable.

■ **5. 'displays any writing, sign or other visible representation which was threatening, abusive or insulting'**
This point means showing any written matter or other visual matter such as a swastika which would threaten, abuse or insult.

■ **6. 'Within the hearing or sight of a person'**

This point means that the offence must be near enough to another person(s) for it to be heard or seen. The 'person' could be a police officer who is caused harassment, alarm or distress, but taking into account all the facts the magistrates might equally decide that the words or behaviour did not have this effect, *DPP v Orum* [1988] 3 All ER 449.

Note the defence shown at point 2 above, when the offender has no reason to believe anyone was within hearing or seeing distances who was likely to be caused harassment, alarm or distress, eg if some people could see him, but they were a long way off. There is a further defence where the accused proves he was inside a dwelling and has no reason to believe his conduct would be heard or seen outside that dwelling or any other dwelling (section 5(3)). It was held in *Chappell v DPP* (1988) 89 Cr App Rep 82 that to deliver through the letter box some writing etc, does not contravene this section because the sender was not a person who 'uses… words or behaviour… within the hearing or sight of a person' who received it.

■ **7. 'likely to be caused harassment, alarm or distress'.**
These terms are not defined and the ordinary meaning should be used. The point means only a likelihood of harassment etc, not an actual harassment. In *Lodge v DPP* (1988) *The Times*, 26 October it was found that it is not necessary that the person alarmed should be concerned at physical danger to himself. Alarm for the safety of an unconnected third party would suffice. Later in *Chambers and Edwards v DPP* [1995] Crim LR 896 it was held that apprehension concerning personal safety was not required for harassment to be established.

(C) USUAL METHODS OF PROVING THESE POINTS
■ **1. 'That you'**
This point is proved by the officer who arrests the suspect stating that the defendant in court is the person involved. Any witness who saw the offence could prove this point.

■ **2. 'did at ....'**

The location of the offence can be proved by the officer in the case to show that the offender could not avail himself of the dwelling defence under section 5(2) and (3).

■ **3. 'use threatening, abusive or insulting words or behaviour'**

This point is best proved by taking a statement from a witness to say that he felt the words or behaviour were threatening, abusive or insulting. A judge has said that the ordinary man knows an insult when he sees or hears one. The mens rea or mental state of the offender must be proved to show an intent or an awareness that his words or behaviour were threatening, abusive or insulting. This could be done by questions and answers such as, 'Did you intend?' or, 'Were you aware etc?'

■ **4. 'or disorderly behaviour'**

This point can be proved by a description in the police officer's statement of evidence such as, 'I saw the accused push into a queue of football supporters' or, 'I saw the accused jumping over flower containers in the Market Place'. If this point is charged or reported then the accused's mental state or mens rea should be proved, ie an intent to be or an awareness that his conduct may be disorderly. Again such points can best be proved by questioning the offender.

■ **5. 'displays any writing, sign or other visible representation which was threatening, abusive or insulting'**

As pointed out, this part of the offence will be rather rare. The point can be proved by describing the display which may entail seizing the articles concerned.

■ **6. 'within the hearing or sight of a person'**

This can be proved by observing the reactions of passers-by or persons to whom the insults etc, were directed, eg, 'I saw two old ladies hurry past looking disgusted and saying, "You ought to be locked up"'.

Better proof would be obtained by taking statements from the 'other' person(s) to say what they saw or heard.

■ **7. 'likely to be caused harassment, alarm or distress'.**

These new words can be proved by taking statements from an aggrieved person(s) to say how harassed, alarmed or distressed he was. Where this is not possible the officer dealing could show in his evidence that it was likely that the other party would be harassed, distressed or alarmed.

(D) SUPPORTING EVIDENCE

As mentioned under (D) of the previous offence (2A Fear or provocation of violence), a police officer may be threatened, abused or insulted. For the purposes of *mens rea* or the mental state of the accused - where the awareness of the accused is impaired by intoxicants - he shall be taken to be aware of that which he would have been aware if not intoxicated, unless he shows either that his intoxication was not self-induced or that it was caused solely by the taking or administration of a substance in the course of medical treatment (section 6(5)).

Note 1. In subsection (5) 'intoxication' means any intoxication, whether caused by drink, drugs or other means, or by a combination of means (section 6(6) Public Order Act 1986).

Note 2. If this offence is racially aggravated, the more serious offence under section 31 of the Crime and Disorder Act 1998 should be considered (see Racial Aggravation Chart at offence 2E).

2C. INTENTION TO CAUSE HARASSMENT, ALARM OR DISTRESS

Section 4A Public Order Act 1986

(See Racial Aggravation Chart at offence 2E.)

(A) POINTS TO PROVE

1. That you 2. did at .... 3. with intent to cause a

person harassment, alarm or distress 4. use threatening, abusive or insulting words or behaviour, or disorderly behaviour or 5. display any writing, sign or other visible representation which was threatening, abusive or insulting namely .... thereby causing that or another person harassment, alarm or distress.

(B) MEANING OF TERMS

■ 1. 'That you'

Means the identity of the offender.

■ 2. 'did at ....'

Means the place where the offence was committed. See (B) 2 of the previous offence.

■ 3. 'with intent to cause a person harassment, alarm or distress '

Means a guilty knowledge or mens rea on the part of the offender. This offence has been designed to remedy persistent racial harassment but it applies equally to other types of harassment. Harassment, alarm or distress are not defined and the normal dictionary definitions will apply.

■ 4. 'use threatening, abusive or insulting words or behaviour, or disorderly behaviour'

See (B) 3 and 4 of the previous offence.

■ 5. 'display any writing, sign or other visible representation which was, threatening, abusive or insulting, namely ....' 'See (B) 5 of the previous offence.

■ 6. 'thereby causing that or another person harassment, alarm or distress'.

This point differs from the previous offence which only requires that the harassment etc is LIKELY to be caused. In this intentional offence the harassment etc must be shown to have been caused. Note that causing harassment etc to another person, other than the one intended to suffer harassment, would suffice for this offence.

(C) USUAL METHODS OF PROVING THESE POINTS

■ 1. 'That you'

Is proved usually by the arresting officer or other witness who saw the offending behaviour.

■ 2. 'did at ....'

The arresting officer or other witness could prove this point. The defence of being inside a dwelling should be borne in mind.

■ 3. 'with intent to cause a person harassment, alarm or distress'

The best proof of intent is from the mouth of the offender, but persistent offending or other circumstantial evidence would suffice. A question such as, 'Did you realise that swastika you displayed would cause distress?' should elicit the intent of the accused.

■ 4. 'use threatening, abusive or insulting words or behaviour, or disorderly behaviour'

See (C)3 and 4 of the previous offence (2B, Conduct likely to cause harassment, alarm or distress).

■ 5. 'display any writing, sign or other visible representation which was threatening, abusive or insulting, namely ....'

This point will be encountered less often than the previous point. Proving it may entail seizing the offending article for evidence and describing the circumstances in the appropriate witness statement. A phrase similar to the following will be necessary, 'I took possession of the swastika banner which was being displayed on the synagogue steps which was obviously threatening to the persons attending the synagogue. I saw two women begin to cry when they saw the swastikas.'

■ 6. 'thereby causing that or another person harassment, alarm or distress'.

Again, this point can be proved from the observation of the arresting officer, or better still from a witness statement made by the offended party. Bear in mind that the person whom the accused originally intended to harass etc need not be the person finally harassed. A statement from the person finally harassed would prove this point.

If this offence is racially aggravated, the more serious offence under section 31 of the Crime and Disorder Act 1998 should be considered (see Racial Aggravation Chart at offence 2E).

2D. STALKING ETC WITHOUT VIOLENCE
Sections 1 and 2 Protection from Harassment Act 1997

(See Racial Aggravation Chart at offence 2E)

(A) POINTS TO PROVE
1. That you 2. pursued 3. a course of conduct 4. on at least two occasions 5. while knowing (or while you ought to have known) 6. that it amounted to harassment 7. of another.

(B) MEANING OF TERMS
■ **1. 'That you'**
Means the identity of the offender.
■ **2. 'pursued'**
The dictionary definition of pursued includes 'follow with intent to capture or kill' but it is likely that the legislators used this word to mean, 'stick to', 'aim at', 'persistently attend', 'continued' (as in continued or pursued a line of inquiry).
■ **3. 'a course of conduct'**
Means the *modus operandi* (method of operation). Nuisance mail, telephone calls, emails, following, photographing etc could all be considered. 'Conduct' includes speech. However, note that there must be a 'course' of conduct, ie an onward movement or pattern of conduct.
■ **4. 'on at least two occasions'**
Means two or more times.

■ 5. 'while knowing (or while you ought to have known)'

This is the offender's *mens rea* (state of mind). It means that the offender knew and understood his or her course of conduct, or should have known and understood the course of conduct. The 'reasonable person' test may be applied here. It can be considered as obvious to the offender that his/her course of conduct amounted to harassment **if a reasonable person in possession of the same information would consider that the course of conduct amounted to harassment of the other**. Therefore the objective test of 'What would a reasonable person have thought?' may be used to determine the accused's state of mind.

■ 6. 'that it amounted to harassment'

Although not defined in the Act, harassment is defined in the dictionary as, to vex by repeated attacks, trouble and worry. Some adverse effect on the victim is necessary. The offender need not intend any harm to the victim. On the contrary, infatuation or hero worship may be the motive. It is generally the unusual or unwanted behaviour of the offender that causes distress etc in the victim.

■ 7. 'of another' Means any person other than the offender.

(C) USUAL METHODS OF PROVING THESE POINTS

■ 1. 'That you'

Identity may be proved by evidence from the victim or witness(es) who saw or heard the offender, or by the arresting officer as this is an arrestable offence. In circumstances in which the victim has never seen the offender, an admission from the suspect is the ideal. The absence of such evidence will necessitate the use of forensic evidence such as DNA samples, fingerprints, handwriting comparison techniques etc.

■ 2. 'pursued'

This can be proved by demonstrating the **repeated** annoyance or distress caused to the victim; or by the **pattern** of behaviour of the offender - the pattern of letters, phone calls, sightings etc.

■ **3. ' a course of conduct'**
Can be proved by showing the *modus operandi* of the offender. Examples would be by taping phone calls, by videoing the offender's presence in the vicinity of the victim's home or when following the victim in the street. A specific example would be to demonstrate the offender's presence on the front row of the theatre at a particularly actor's every performance, and then pestering the actor at the stage door.

■ **4. 'on at least two occasions'**
The prosecution must prove that course of conduct was pursued more than once.

■ **5. 'while knowing (or while you ought to have known)'**
This *mens rea* can be proved in the officer's interview, by the offender admitting knowledge of the distress caused, or from the inference that a reasonable person would have thought the course of conduct amounted to harassment when presented with the facts.

■ **6. 'that it amounted to harassment'**
Can be proved by the victim's statement, showing that he or she was in a state of mind somewhere between worry and terror due to the offender's course of conduct.

■ **7. 'of another'**
Proved by identifying the victim in his or her statement and may be from an admission by the accused.

(D) SUPPORTING EVIDENCE

Note 1. Defences to this offence are available where the suspect shows that (on the balance of probabilities) the course of conduct was pursued:

    (a)   for the purpose of preventing or detecting crime;

    (b)   under any enactment or rule of law, or to comply with any condition or requirement imposed by any person under any enactment; or

    (c)   in such a manner as to be reasonable.

Examples of the above may include the activities of private detectives or county court bailiffs etc during the course of their duties.

Note 2. Where this offence is racially aggravated, the more serious offence under section 32 of the Crime and Disorder Act 1998 is committed (see the Racial Aggravation Chart at offence 2E).

Note 3. Also consider the offence of Harassment with fear of violence under section 4 of the Protection from Harassment Act 1997.

Note 4. This offence is to be preferred to the 'offensive telephone calls offence' at offence 4 because it carries a power of entry to arrest under PACE.

Where the stalking offence involves a telephone (mobile or otherwise), the power of entry to arrest is available if necessary. Most of the new telephone companies have police liaison officers and 'nuisance' call departments. Improved technology has made it easier to bug/intercept and trace nuisance callers, but follow your own force instructions/procedures in this sensitive area.

2E. RACIALLY AGGRAVATED OFFENCES
Crime and Disorder Act 1998

(See Racial Aggravation Chart overleaf)

(A) POINTS TO PROVE
(a) 1. At the time of committing the offence, or immediately before or after doing so 2. the offender demonstrates towards the victim of the offence 3. hostility 4. based on the victim's membership (or presumed membership) 5. of a racial group; or

(b) 6. the offence is motivated (wholly or partly) by hostility towards members of a racial group based on their membership of that group.

RACIAL AGGRAVATION CHART

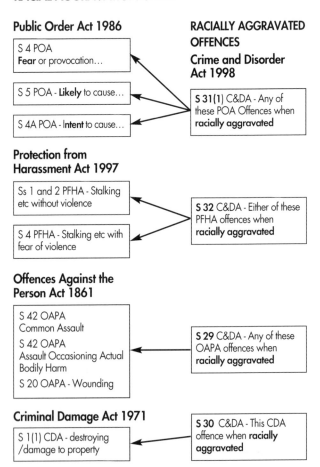

Public Order Act 1986

S 4 POA
Fear or provocation...

S 5 POA - **Likely** to cause...

S 4A POA - **Intent** to cause...

RACIALLY AGGRAVATED OFFENCES
Crime and Disorder Act 1998

S 31(1) C&DA - Any of these POA Offences when **racially aggravated**

Protection from Harassment Act 1997

Ss 1 and 2 PFHA - Stalking etc without violence

S 4 PFHA - Stalking etc with fear of violence

S 32 C&DA - Either of these PFHA offences when **racially aggravated**

Offences Against the Person Act 1861

S 42 OAPA
Common Assault

S 42 OAPA
Assault Occasioning Actual Bodily Harm

S 20 OAPA - Wounding

S 29 C&DA - Any of these OAPA offences when **racially aggravated**

Criminal Damage Act 1971

S 1(1) CDA - destroying /damage to property

S 30 C&DA - This CDA offence when **racially aggravated**

(B) MEANING OF TERMS

■ 1. At the time of committing the offence, or immediately before or after doing so

The term 'immediately' is not defined but the further in time between the hostility and the offence - either before or after - the less chance there is of 'racial aggravation' being proved.

Help may be gleaned from Robbery (offence 20) which uses 'immediately before' and the offence of Robbery under previous legislation which uses before and afterwards.

■ 2. the offender demonstrates towards the victim of the offence

'Demonstrates towards' is the *actus reus* or the guilty act and could include actions, writing, signs, visible representations or speech. 'Towards' requires that the demonstration to be directed specifically at the victim rather than to be a general demonstration.

■ 3. hostility

This means unfriendly, opposition, enmity to an outright state of warfare according to the dictionary definition. Some hostility will have an obvious root in racial or religious confrontation; other types may be more subtle and harder to prove, such as attacks on economic immigrants.

■ 4. based on the victim's membership (or presumed membership)

'Membership or presumed membership' means a 'belonging' to a group. This for example may be the obvious belonging of persons of full African decent or the less obvious membership of persons of half or quarter blood relationship.

This will be for the courts to decide but the Act helps by including persons who merely associate with such groups (eg the white girlfriend of a coloured man) and also including those who the offender presumes to be a member of a group, even if the presumption is mistaken (eg an ethnic Italian who was presumed to be Asian).

■ 5. of a racial group

Racial group means a group of persons defined by reference to race, colour, nationality (including citizenship) or ethnic or national origins. For example, Sikhs, Jews and Romany gypsies may be considered to be racial groups.

However, groups defined solely by religious, political, or cultural characteristics, such as Ratafarians, Communists, Mormons or New Age travellers, do not fall within the definition.

■ 6. the offence is motivated (wholly or partly) by hostility towards members of a racial group based on their membership of that group.

'Motivated', in this context, is the state of mind of the offender (the *mens rea*). In (a)1.-5. above a 'demonstration' of individual hostility is required, while as (b)6. the 'motive' is required.

Take the offence of common assault on a black person as an example. If the phrase 'black bastard' was used immediately before, during or immediately after the assault, then (b)1.-5. above would apply. However, consider a group of persons who 'wholly or partly' hated black people and attacked a group of Asians without any obvious 'demonstration' of hostility based on race. This 'motive' or *mens reas* is a much more difficult concept to prove.

(C) USUAL METHODS OF PROVING THESE POINTS

■ 1. At the time of committing the offence, or immediately before or after doing so

This is proved by the offender admitting, or the victim or other witness(es) stating when the hostility took place. In cases which involve telephone call, emails, photographs etc, then other methods may be appropriate.

■ 2. the offender demonstrates towards the victim of the offence

'Demonstrates towards' is proved by showing the offender's actions, either physical, verbal or written. The victim's or other witness(es)' statements would include the *actus reas*.

■ 3. hostility

The particularly hostile act would be described by the offender and/or the witnesses. For example a Nazi salute to a Jew, verbal abuse of a black person or written abuse to an Asian.

■ 4. based on the victim's membership (or presumed membership)

This would be best evidenced by a description and explanation in the victim's statement. For example 'My parents are both Asian Indians and I am Indian in appearance. At the time of the offence, I was wearing Indian dress (give description) and a turban which is associated with being a Sikh… etc.' This could be backed by witness(es)'s description plus the observations of the officer in the case.

In cases in which the offender has rightly or wrongly **assumed** membership, then the outward manifestations could be proved by witnesses, or the inward belief during the course of the interview/taped interview/statement under caution etc with the defendant.

Where 'association' with a racial group is a necessary point to prove, then statements from the person associating, and from a member of the group associated with, would be required. For example, 'I have all white Scottish ancestry and have been the girl-friend of Ramjit Singh, an ethnic Asian, for four years'; plus 'I am the sister of Ramjit Singh and have known Christine for four years as she has visited our house most weeks over this period of time.'

■ 5. of a racial group

Proof of race, colour, nationality (including citizenship), or ethnic or national origins could be by a statement from the victim, or from an embassy or consul official, passport details etc.

No doubt case law will develop the definition of 'racial group' and officers should keep themselves aware of additions to, or deletions from, the group. (Membership of a group by association and mistaken presumption of membership by the offender are as described above at point 4.)

■ 6. the offence is motivated (wholly or partly) by hostility towards members of a racial group based on their membership of that group.

This is part (b) of the two part offence. Part (a) 1.-5. requires demonstrated hostility to the victim, and this part (b)6 requires motivation by hostility towards a racial group.

It is considered that the majority of circumstances would fall into the easier to prove (a)1.-5.

However, if it in necessary to prove (b)6. then the problems of proving a state of mind are encountered. Best evidence would be an outright admission by the accused that he or she was motivated (wholly or partly) by hostility towards the racial group. This could form part of a comment after being cautioned, part of a taped interview or part of a statement under caution.

Failing such an admission, then circumstantial evidence may suffice. Examples would be evidence of what the accused had said to close friends or relatives, the accused's actions, evidence of similar facts, previous conduct or conduct post the offence.

BUILDING GOOD RACE RELATIONS

A proactive check-list for constables
based on the Macpherson Report recommendations

- Do know the Ministerial Priority for all the Police Service: 'To increase trust and confidence in policing among minority ethnic communities' (recommendation 1).
- Do know the definition of 'racist incident': 'A racist incident is any incident which is perceived to be racist by the victim or any other person' (recommendation 12).
  Note that the subjective perception of the definition depends on what is in the mind of the victim or any other person.

Their perception can be established from comments such as: 'I felt the graffiti to be racist as it said, "Go home", and although my parents and I were born in England, our colour attracts such comments', from the victim; OR 'I felt sorry for my neighbours as such racist graffiti must upset them even though their family has lived in England for 40 years', from 'any other person'.

Once an incident is classed as 'racist' then records and prioritisation can take place.

■ Do know your force's key performance indicators to help implement, monitor and assess the Ministerial Priority (recommendation 2).

■ Do know your force's strategy to:
Prevent; Investigate; Record, and Prosecute
racist incidents.

■ Do know what your force is doing to encourage the reporting of racist incidents (recommendation 16).

■ Do be aware of the numbers of racist incidents and the detection levels in your area (recommendation 15).

■ Do keep abreast of:
- multi-agency co-operation;
- information exchange;
- surveys to show levels of equal satisfaction in all ethnic groups.

■ Do know your family/witness/victim/liaison officers (recommendation 23).

■ Do take full part in any racist awareness training and cultivate your own knowledge continuously. Appreciate the value and positive aspects of cultural diversity eg food, dress, religion, family ties etc (recommendation 48).

■ Do know the level of complaints of racist behaviour/attitude in your force and the outcomes (rec 55).

▌ Do keep your first aid training up-to-date and practise continually (not just at exam time) (rec 45).

▌ Do know the position in your local schools regarding the 'promotion of cultural diversity' as a positive issue; the number of racist incidents (if any) and other school and educational initiatives in this field (rec 67).

Behaviours for constables to avoid
based on common sense

▌ Avoid racist, sexist or homophobic behaviour/attitudes in work or domestic and social life.

▌ Do not encourage racist humour.

▌ Take care not to adversely misinterpret language or body language from persons having different cultural backgrounds than your own.

▌ Do not be impatient towards, intolerant of or too ready to criticise ethnic minorities, or indeed anyone else.

▌ Do not associate yourself with racist people either in your work, your social life, or at venues you may attend such as sporting events, concerts, demonstrations etc.

In conclusion...
Remember that Britain is a diverse and multi-racial society. By reducing and eradicating racism much individual misery will disappear and valuable time and money will be released to fund other crucial areas of policing.

3. INDECENT EXPOSURE
Common law, Vagrancy Act 1824 and Town Police Clauses Act 1847

3A. INDECENT EXPOSURE
Common law

(A) POINTS TO PROVE
1. That you 2. did unlawfully, wilfully and 3. publicly expose 4. your naked person.

(B) MEANING OF TERMS
■ **1. 'That you'**
Means the identity of the person exposing himself or herself.
■ **2. 'did unlawfully, wilfully and'**
This point means intentionally as opposed to accidentally and unlawfully as opposed to lawfully such as an artist's model.
■ **3. 'publicly expose'**
Publicly means an exposure which can be seen by more than one person. Men and women can commit this offence and it need not be in a public place.
■ **4. 'your naked person'.**
Means, in most of the reported cases, the naked penis although it may well be that exposure of the vagina would be within the mischief the offence is trying to prevent.

(C) USUAL METHODS OF PROVING THESE POINTS
■ **1. 'That you'**
Proof of the identity of an accused exposing his/her person may be difficult and, without an admission, a witness is required to say that the man/woman in the court dock is the person who exposed their person.
■ **2. 'did unlawfully, wilfully and'**
This point will depend on the circumstances of each case. However, if the accused has done the same act on a number of occasions, and if he admits he did it intentionally or if he draws attention to himself etc, then unlawful and wilful conduct may be proved.

■ **3. 'publicly exposes'**
Proof of 'publicly' is by showing that the exposure was to more than one person. This offence can be committed in a private place, *Ford v Falcone* [1971] 2 All ER 1138.

■ **4. 'your naked person'.**
Proved by witness statement(s) showing that the person was not covered.

(D) SUPPORTING EVIDENCE

Note. This offence is rarely used as it can only be tried on indictment. If the circumstances of the offence constitute a common law public nuisance the Criminal Law Act 1977 allows for trial either way.

3B. INDECENT EXPOSURE
Section 4 Vagrancy Act 1824

(A) POINTS TO PROVE
1. That you 2. did wilfully, openly, lewdly and obscenely 3. expose your person 4. with intent to insult a certain female named ....

(B) MEANING OF TERMS

■ **1. 'That you'**
Means the identity of the person exposing himself.

■ **2. 'did wilfully, openly, lewdly and obscenely'**
This point means, without concealment and usually involves an erect penis as opposed to a man merely urinating.

■ **3. 'expose your person'**
Means the penis. No other part of the body will suffice for this offence.

■ **4. 'with intent to insult a certain female named ....'.**
This point means that the accused must have intended to insult a female. It rules out any accidental exposure and exposing to males.

(C) USUAL METHODS OF PROVING THESE POINTS

■ **1. 'That you'** See (C)1 of offence 3A.

■ **2. 'did wilfully, openly, lewdly and obscenely'**
These terms are proved by a witness stating the penis was exposed openly and not accidentally and that it was erect, stiff or swollen etc, The accused may admit the exposure was wilful etc, verbally and or by making a statement under caution.

■ **3. 'expose your person'**
Proved by describing the penis fully and stating its condition as point 2 above. An experienced woman usually has no difficulty, but children or young women should be definite in what they have seen. Fingers, hernias and extended navels have caused problems in practice when the defence has submitted that it was not the penis which was exposed but some similar-looking object.

Note that justices may convict where it can be inferred that at the material time, the penis was exposed. This is so even when there is no direct evidence that the male organ was seen by a witness, *Hunt v DPP* [1990] Crim LR 812.

■ **4. 'with intent to insult a certain female named ....'.**
The intent can best be proved by an admission from the accused or what he said to the female to whom he exposed himself. Circumstantial evidence may be used and so may evidence of similar conduct. Evidence could be called to prove a similar course of conduct towards other females where a defence of accident or mistake is put forward, *Perkins v Jeffrey* [1915] 5 KB 702.

3C. INDECENT EXPOSURE
Section 28 Town Police Clauses Act 1847

(A) POINTS TO PROVE
1. That you 2. did in a certain street called .... 3. to the annoyance of the residents (or passengers) 4. wilfully and indecently 5. expose your person.

(B) MEANING OF TERMS
■ **1. 'That you'**
The identity of the person exposing himself.
■ **2. 'did in a certain street called ....'**
'Street' includes any road, square, court, alley and thoroughfare or public passage (section 8 Town Police Clauses Act 1847). A street is also deemed to be any place of public resort or recreation ground belonging to, or under the control of, the local authority and any unfenced ground adjoining or abutting upon any street in an urban district (section 81 Public Health Acts Amendment Act 1907).

In *Mantle v Jordan* [1961] JP 119, it was held that, although the offence must be committed in the 'street' the annoyance may be to 'residents', ie the occupants of houses in the street who need not be out of their houses 'in the street' at the time of the offence.
■ **3. 'to the annoyance of the residents (or passengers)'**
'Annoyance' would seem to be a question of degree for the court to decide. It would appear that residents live in the street and passengers use the street,
■ **4. 'wilfully and indecently'**
Means wilfully as opposed to accidentally or mistakenly and against normal standards of decency.
■ **5. 'expose your person'.** Means exposes the penis.

(C) USUAL METHODS OF PROVING THESE POINTS
■ **1. 'That you'** See (C)1 of offence 3A.
■ **2. 'did in a certain street called ....'**
This point can be proved by the constable dealing with the case describing the place sufficiently for it to come within the definition of 'street' at (B)2 of this offence.
■ **3. 'to the annoyance of the residents (or passengers)'**
'Annoyance' can be proved by the person(s) to whom the exposure was made, explaining their feelings of annoyance in their

evidence. Such person(s) should also state whether they were residents or passengers.

(Police officers who, following complaints, had been stationed at a block of public conveniences and saw the defendant masturbating, were held not to be 'passengers', *Cheeseman v DPP* [1991] Crim LR 296.)

■ **4. 'wilfully and indecently'**

'Wilfully' can be proved from the accused's own admission or from his comments or actions at the time of the offence. Indecently can be shown by the penis being erect and any other point that will negate any possible defence of accident or mistake.

■ **5. 'expose your person'.**

This point is proved by the person(s) to whom the exposure was made, explaining in detail what they saw etc,

(D) SUPPORTING EVIDENCE

There is no requirement to prove 'intent to insult a female' in this offence as there is in the Vagrancy Act offences.

4. TELEPHONE CALLS - OFFENSIVE ETC
Section 43(1) Telecommunications Act 1984

(A) POINTS TO PROVE

1. That you 2. did send a message by telephone which was grossly offensive, or 3. send a message by telephone which was of an indecent (or an obscene or a menacing) character or 4. send a message by telephone to .... (specify person) which you knew to be false for the purpose of causing annoyance (or inconvenience or needless anxiety) to the said .... (or to ....) or 5. persistently make telephone calls without reasonable cause and for the purpose of causing annoyance (or inconvenience or needless anxiety) to ....

(B) MEANING OF TERMS

■ 1. 'That you'
Means the identity of the person making the obscene etc, calls.

■ 2. 'did send a message by telephone which was grossly offensive, or'
Means the message must have gone by a public telecommunication system and must be very offensive.

'Telecommunication system' means a system for the conveyance - through the agency of electric, magnetic, electro-magnetic, electro-chemical or electro-mechanical energy - of:

(a) speech, music and other sounds;

(b) visual images;

(c) signals serving for the impartation (whether as between persons and persons, things and things, or persons and things) of any matter otherwise than in the form of sounds or visual images; or

(d) signals serving for the actuation/control of machinery/apparatus.

Telecommunication apparatus which is situated in the UK and:

(a) is connected to but not comprised within a telecommunication system; or

(b) is connected to and comprised in a telecommunication system which extends beyond the United Kingdom;

shall be regarded as a telecommunication system, and any person who controls the apparatus shall be regarded as running the system.

Such offensive calls are usually of a sexual nature, eg heavy breathers, and also come under point 3. However, they could be offensive in other ways, such as telling a woman that her husband was having an affair, was homosexual or had a criminal record.

■ 3. 'send a message by telephone which was of an indecent (or an obscene or a menacing) character or'
'Telephone' means the same public system as at the alternative point at 2 above. Indecent and obscene are usually in the form of heavy breathing, or suggestions of an obscene sexual nature etc. Menacing calls include threats of violence to the person or property.

■ **4 & 5. These points are similar to points 2 and 3 above but vary slightly in the content of the call.**

For point 4, examples would include falsely telling a woman her husband was dead or that he was having an affair. Point 5 includes action such as needlessly ringing a telephone in the early hours of the morning.

(C) USUAL METHODS OF PROVING THESE POINTS
■ **1. 'That you'**

When the offender is on the other end of a telephone this point is usually difficult to prove. Apart from an admission, the prosecution have to rely on catching the offender redhanded by keeping observations on a suspect or by a telephone company official tracing a persistent caller when he is actually making a call etc, or by the recipient having a system which displays the number of an incoming call. The recipient could also give evidence that she recognised the voice or tape recorded the offender.

■ **2. 'did send a message by telephone which was grossly offensive or'**

As with the last point the telephone causes problems. The receiver of the call could give evidence that the grossly offensive message was received on a public telephone.

■ **3. 'send a message by telephone which was of an indecent (or an obscene or a menacing) character, or'**

This point is proved as the last point with the recipient explaining the indecent, obscene or menacing nature of the call.

■ **4 & 5.** These points are proved as the last two points.

(D) SUPPORTING EVIDENCE

Note. The recent massive increase in the use of mobile phones has led to large numbers of 'nuisance' calls. To combat this most of the phone companies have appointed 'police liaison' officers' and set up 'nuisance' calls departments. Improved technology is helping to increase detection rates and the new offence of Stalking (see offence 2D) is making the investigation of 'nuisance' calls easier by providing a power of entry to arrest under PACE (unlike this Telecommunications Act offence).

5. OFFENSIVE WEAPON
Section 1(1) Prevention of Crime Act 1953

(A) POINTS TO PROVE
1. That you 2. without lawful authority or reasonable excuse 3. had with you 4. in a public place called ....
5. an offensive weapon namely a ....

(B) MEANING OF TERMS
■ 1. 'That you'
Means the identity of the person who had the offensive weapon with him.
■ 2. 'without lawful authority or reasonable excuse'
Lawful authority means the lawful carrying of the weapon such as a policeman's truncheon. The lawful carrying of something like a car jack which is used to cause injury on the spur of the moment does not necessarily make it an offensive weapon (*R v Dayle* [1973] 3 All ER 1151).

The prosecution are safer trying to show some interval of time between forming the intent to use the article to injure and the actual use. Reasonable excuse may be found where a person carries a weapon as self-protection from imminent attack (*Evans v Hughes* [1972] 3 All ER 412). Carrying a knife on the off chance of being attacked, and weapons carried by dance hall security guards have been held not to be a reasonable excuse.
■ 3. 'had with you'
This point means that the accused must have known he had the weapon with him (*R v Cugullere* [1961] 2 All ER 343).

Constructive possession, ie at his house or any place when the accused is not there, is not sufficient.

■ **4. 'in a public place called ....'**

'Public place' includes any highway and any other premises or place to which at the material time the public have or are permitted to have access whether on payment or otherwise (section 1(4) Prevention of Crime Act 1953). In *R v Mehmed* [1963] Crim LR 780 where the accused had an air pistol which he produced in another's private house, it would be reasonable to assume that he must have carried it in a public place to get it there or to take it away. It was open to the court to make this inference.

■ **5. 'an offensive weapon namely a ....'.**

Offensive weapon means any article made or adapted for use for causing injury to the person or intended by the person having it with him for such use by him, or by some other person, per section 1(4) Prevention Of Crime Act 1953 as amended by the Public Order Act 1986 Schedule 2, paragraph 2. Therefore three categories exist, ie (i) made; (ii) adapted; or (iii) intended.

Examples of 'made' include a knuckleduster or bayonet. Examples of 'adapted' include a bottle specially broken to use as a weapon, or a belt if it has been specially studded for use as a weapon. Examples of an article 'intended' for use as an offensive weapon include a dart which the accused intends to throw in a football crowd or a pocket full of stones which the accused intends to throw at members of a rival demonstration.

An intent to cause injury by shock is sufficient and apparently means the same as an intent to cause injury to the person (*R v Rapier* [1980] Crim LR 48).

(C) USUAL METHODS OF PROVING THESE POINTS

■ **1. 'That you'**

Can be proved by the officer dealing with the case proving an admission by the accused that he was the person concerned.

Any witness who saw the incident and could identify the accused could prove this point.

■ 2. 'without lawful authority or reasonable excuse'

The proof of this point is on the defence and they must prove on the balance of probabilities that the accused had it with him with lawful authority or reasonable excuse. It is advisable for the prosecution to anticipate any such defence and try to negate any fraudulent defence at the investigation stage.

■ 3. 'had with you'

This point is proved by the police officer or other witness stating, 'He held the dart in his hand' or, 'The knuckleduster was visible sticking out of his jacket pocket', etc. The defence could always allege only a constructive possession and that there was no actual possession in the absence of a witness stating positive actual possession.

■ 4. 'in a public place called ....'

Proof must be available that the offence occurred at a place coming within the definition at point (B)4 of this offence. Note that the court could infer that the accused had been in a public place where no such direct evidence exists. (See point (B)4, *R v Mehmed*.)

■ 5. 'an offensive weapon namely a ....'.

Proof of an offensive weapon depends on which of the three categories, outlined at point (B)5 of this offence, is used.

If 'made' or 'adapted' is used the prosecution need only prove that the accused had it with him. They need not prove that the accused had it with him with the intention of using it to cause injury to the person. This proof is only required when the 'intended' category is used.

Therefore where an otherwise innocent article is concerned it can only become an offensive weapon if the accused intended to use it to cause personal injury. This can be proved by comments from the accused to the effect, 'I carried it to use in case I was ever attacked'. The case of *R v Dayle* outlined at (B)2 shows that the offence is 'had with him' and not 'picked up on the spur of the moment'. The prosecution should try to prove an interval of time between forming the intention and using the article to injure when the third category of 'intended' is used (*Ohlson v Hylton* [1975] 2 All ER 490).

(D) SUPPORTING EVIDENCE

Flick knives have caused problems in the past when trying to decide whether they are offensive weapons by themselves (without having to prove the intent of the possessor to use them for causing injury). The position is clearer since *Gibson v Wales* [1983] Crim LR 113. In this case police officers saw the defendant take a flick knife from his pocket and give it to a friend to inspect before returning it to his pocket. The police did not prove any intent on the part of the possessor to use it to cause injury.

The Queen's Bench Divisional Court held that a flick knife was an offensive weapon by itself, ie made for the purpose of causing injury to the person. Therefore flick knives are now in the same category as truncheons and knuckledusters.

In practice, although the prosecution can now rely on the mere possession of a flick knife, it would be wise to prove an intent to injure where this is possible.

6. ASSAULT OCCASIONING ACTUAL BODILY HARM (AOABH)

Section 47 Offences Against the Person Act 1861

(A) POINTS TO PROVE

1. That you 2. did assault .... (specify person)
3. thereby occasioning him actual bodily harm.

(B) MEANING OF TERMS

■ 1. 'That you' Means the identity of the accused.

■ **2. 'did assault .... (specify person)'**
Proof is required of an assault which occasioned actual bodily harm. The prosecution are not obliged to prove that the defendant intended to cause some actual bodily harm or was reckless as to whether such harm would be caused.

■ **3. 'thereby occasioning him actual bodily harm'.**
Means a hurt or injury which is more serious than a common assault and less serious than an unlawful wounding chargeable under section 20 Offences against the Person Act 1861 (permanent disability or disfigurement). Examples of actual bodily harm include lost teeth, extensive bruising, minor fractures, loss of consciousness.

An assault causing a psychiatric or nervous condition is also sufficient (*R v Miller* [1954] 2 QB 282), as are strange telephone calls if they make the victim apprehensive and cause psychological damage (*R v Ireland* [1997] 161 JP 569 HL). Where pain is alleged as a result of a non-physical assault the court must have psychiatric evidence of whether the conduct could have caused the injury. *R v Morris* [1998] Cr App Rep 386.

The assault must occasion the bodily harm.

(C) USUAL METHODS OF PROVING THESE POINTS

■ **1. 'That you'** The identity of the accused can be proved by the evidence of the victim or an admission etc.

■ **2. 'did assault ....'**
'Assault' is proved by showing the accused's actions come within the definition of assault at (B)2 of this offence. In most cases there will be physical contact between the accused and his victim and this can be proved by any person who witnessed the offence.

Where an assault cannot be proved, an offence of unlawful wounding or inflicting grievous bodily harm contrary to section 20 of the Offences against the Person Act 1861 can be considered. Where the injury is very minor then common assault under section 39 Criminal Justice Act 1988 should be considered. See offence 6A.

■ 3. 'thereby occasioning him actual bodily harm'.

This point is proved by describing the injury sustained by the victim, eg, 'He had several bruises about 4cm in diameter on his face'. Photographic and/or medical evidence could be considered if it is thought that the injuries would be difficult to prove. The statement made by the victim should also contain a description of the injury. Any medical examination report by a police surgeon or the victim's own doctor etc may be required.

6A COMMON ASSAULT

Contrary to section 39 Criminal Justice Act 1988

(A) POINTS TO PROVE

1. That you 2. did assault by beating or 3. intentionally or recklessly caused .... (enter name of person assaulted) to fear that he would be immediately subjected to 4. unlawful violence.

(B) MEANING OF TERMS

■ 1. 'That you'

Means the identity of the person who assaulted the victim.

■ 2. 'did assault by beating'

Means that an injury was inflicted on the victim, but note that a section 39 offence should only be charged if the injury was trivial, eg grazes or scratches, otherwise a section 47 Offences against the Person Act 1861 offence (assault occasioning actual bodily harm) should be charged (see offence 6).

■ 3. 'intentionally or recklessly cause .... to fear that he would be immediately subjected to

Means that the victim feared the violence would occur right then, therefore the accused must have been physically in a position to use violence against the victim.

■ **4. 'unlawful violence'**

Means that the accused was not acting lawfully, eg prevention of crime, effecting arrest or lawful chastisement of a child by a parent or someone acting in *loco parentis* (or a teacher, but generally only in a private school, not a state school, where corporal punishment is prohibited).

(C) USUAL METHODS OF PROVING THESE POINTS

■ **1. 'That you'**

This is proved by the victim or witnesses to the assault and by questioning the suspect.

■ **2. 'did assault'**

Witness statements and the interview evidence should cover the definition of assault by battery as at (B) above. For example: 'I saw a man I know to be Peter Shepherd hit my husband on his nose with the clenched fist of his right hand....' 'I saw his nose was red and swollen.'

■ **3. intentionally or recklessly caused .... (enter name of person assaulted) to fear that he would be immediately subjected to**

Witnesses would explain the behaviour which made the victim fear that an assault was about to be made upon him.

■ **4. 'unlawful violence'**

This can by proved by showing that the accused had no right in law to assault the victim (see defences in (D) below).

(D) SUPPORTING EVIDENCE

Note 1. Certain defences are available to this offence. If raised it is for the prosecution to counter them. 'Consent' is such a defence, eg a blow struck in a game of rugby, if not likely or intended to cause bodily harm, would usually be lawful as the participants give their tacit consent to the rough and tumble of the game, but extreme behaviour would not be deemed to have received consent. 'Moderate correction' will be a defence for chastising a child and it will be for the prosecution to prove that the accused did more than inflict moderate correction. 'Justification' for an assault may be claimed when done in self-defence, as a response to provocation during the resistance of violence in defence of someone else or in defence of property etc.

Note 2. This offence under section 39 has replaced section 42 Offences against the Person Act 1861 (common assault) which has been repealed. As a consequence it is now improper to advise complainants in domestic violence cases to take their own action and pursue a prosecution under section 42. There is no power of arrest under section 39 but an arrest could be made for the arrestable offence of section 47, AOABH (offence 6) where the victim alleges actual bodily harm has been caused or for breach of the peace. A section 39 offence is dealt with only at a magistrates' court.

7. ASSAULT ON POLICE
Section 89(1) Police Act 1996

(A) POINTS TO PROVE
1. That you 2. did assault .... (specify officer), a constable of the .... Police Force (or Constabulary) 3. in the execution of his/her duty.

(B) MEANING OF TERMS
■ 1. 'That you'
Means the identity of the person who assaulted a constable.
■ 2. 'did assault .... (specify officer), a constable of the .... Police Force (or Constabulary)'
Assault means an act which intentionally or recklessly causes another person to apprehend immediate and unlawful personal violence (*Fagan v Metropolitan Police Commissioner* [1968] 3 All ER 445).

■ 3. 'in the execution of his/her duty'

Means duties connected with protecting life and property, preventing and detecting crime and keeping the peace. The constable must not be exceeding his authority, such as detaining a person where he has no power of arrest. He must not act unlawfully in other ways such as remaining on premises after being lawfully requested to leave.

(C) USUAL METHODS OF PROVING THESE POINTS

■ 1. 'That you'

Can be proved by the officer who has been assaulted giving evidence of identification.

■ 2. 'did assault .... (specify officer) a constable of the .... Police Force (or Constabulary)'

Assault must be proved in accordance with the definition at point (B)2 of this offence. In most cases the accused will strike the officer who should describe the assault in detail. Photographs can be considered in cases where problems are foreseen.

■ 3. 'in the execution of his/her duty'.

Can be proved by describing the duty being performed, eg, 'I said to John Brown "You are being arrested for conduct likely to cause a breach of the peace" and was about to hold his arm and caution him when he struck me in the face with his left fist etc'. If there is any doubt about being able to prove this point successfully the prosecution should consider other offences.

Where any actual bodily harm is occasioned section 47 of the Offences against the Person Act 1861 may be appropriate (see offence 6 ante). Sections 18 and 20 of the same Act can also be considered where there is a wounding or grievous bodily harm, with or without intent.

(D) SUPPORTING EVIDENCE

Note 1. There is no power of arrest for assaulting a constable but consider using the arrest powers under 'breach of the 'peace', Public Order Act 1986 offences, or the conditional powers under section 25 PACE.

Note 2. Also be aware of the offence of assaulting a person assisting a constable.

8. OBSTRUCTING POLICE
Section 89(2) Police Act 1996

(A) POINTS TO PROVE
1. That you 2. did wilfully obstruct (or resist) .... a constable of the .... Police Force (or Constabulary) 3. acting in the execution of his/her duty.

(B) MEANING OF TERMS
■ 1. 'That you'
Means the identity of the person obstructing the police.
■ 2. 'did wilfully obstruct (or resist) .... a constable of the .... Police Force (or Constabulary)'
Wilful obstruction means a deliberate, intentional act which makes it more difficult for the police officer to carry out his/her duty. Examples include warning someone so as to render police investigation fruitless (*Hinchcliffe v Sheldon* [1955] 1 WLR 1207) and drinking alcohol after driving to frustrate the breath test procedure (*Ingleton v Dibble* [1972] 1 QB 480).
■ 3. 'acting in the execution of his/her duty'.
See (B)3 of offence 7.

(C) USUAL METHODS OF PROVING THESE POINTS
■ 1. 'That you'
The officer obstructed should give evidence to identify the accused.
■ 2. 'did wilfully obstruct (or resist) .... a constable of the .... Police Force (or Constabulary)'
This point can be proved by the officer concerned describing

the obstruction in detail, eg, 'I saw John Jones signal to several car drivers to reduce their speed before passing the police operated speed check' etc. Care should be taken by the prosecution to show the obstruction was deliberate and intentional to negate any defence of accident or mistake.

■ **3. 'acting in the execution of his/her duty'.**
See (C)3 of offence 7.

(D) SUPPORTING EVIDENCE

Note 1. There is no specific power of arrest for this offence but see the comments at 'D' of the previous offence.
Note 2. Also be aware of the offence of obstructing someone assisting a constable.

9. INDECENT ASSAULT ON WOMAN
Section 14(1) Sexual Offences Act 1956

(A) POINTS TO PROVE
1. That you 2. did indecently 3. assault .... 4. a woman (or girl under the age of 16 (or 13) years).

(B) MEANING OF TERMS
■ **1. 'That you'**
Means the identity of the person indecently assaulting the woman or girl.
■ **2. 'did indecently'**
'Indecent' means any affront to modesty, usually touching a female's private parts, but less obvious acts include a kiss followed by a suggestion concerning intercourse. To place a finger into the vagina of a girl under 16 years is an indecent assault as there can be no consent to indecent assault under 16 years (*R v McCormack* [1969] 2 QB 442).

■ **3. 'assault ....'**
Means an act which intentionally or recklessly causes another person to apprehend immediate and unlawful personal violence (*Fagan v Metropolitan Police Commissioner* [1968] 3 All ER 445). Note that a hostile touching can be an assault and battery.

■ **4. 'a woman (or girl under the age of 16 (or 13) years)'.**
Although not essential, it is good drafting practise, and of help to the court to show that the victim was under 16 or under 13 years of age.

(C) USUAL METHODS OF PROVING THESE POINTS
■ **1. 'That you'**
This point is proved by the victim giving evidence of identification. Such evidence as saliva and seminal fluid tests, footprints or fingerprints may be helpful. Note that although not required in law, corroboration of the victim's evidence is looked for in practice. Therefore the prosecution should try to provide corroboration for her allegation at the investigation stage, even regarding the accused's identity (*R v Midwinter* (1971) 55 Cr App R 523).

■ **2. 'did indecently'**
The indecent act must be described by the victim in her evidence. Any conversation with or comments made by the accused may help to prove that his actions were prompted by an indecent motive.

■ **3. 'assault ....'**
'Assault' must be proved to fall within the definition at (B)3 of this offence. There will normally be a hostile touching but in the case of *R v Rolfe* (1952) 36 Cr App R 4, a man was convicted of indecent assault without touching the victim. He exposed himself in a railway carriage and moved towards the victim, inviting her to have connections with him.

■ **4. 'a woman (or girl under the age of 16 (or 13) years)'.**
'Age' can sometimes be difficult to prove, but most courts accept

a birth certificate. If problems are anticipated a statement from someone who witnessed the birth is good evidence. A *bona fide* belief that the victim was 16 or over when the indecent assault took place will not amount to a defence (*R v Maughan* (1934) 24 Cr App R 130).

(D) SUPPORTING EVIDENCE

Corroboration is looked for in practice (but is not essential, section 32 Criminal Justice and Public Order Act 1994) and the following circumstances will usually amount to corroboration:

(i) evidence of contact between the accused and the victim on their bodies and clothing;

(ii) the distressed condition of the victim;

(iii) evidence of similar misconduct can be admitted as corroboration if from an independent source;

(iv) the sworn evidence of a child victim can be corroborated by the evidence of another child victim of similar misconduct.

The early complaint of the victim will provide good evidence of credibility but will not amount to corroboration unless an independent source is involved.

Note. Where the accused invites a woman to touch him indecently there can be no offence as there is no assault. But consider the Indecency with Children Act 1960 for children under 14 years who are so invited.

10. SOLICITING FOR PROSTITUTION
Section 1 Street Offences Act 1959

(A) POINTS TO PROVE
1. That you 2. being a common prostitute 3. did loiter (or solicit) 4. in a street (or public place) called .... 5. for the purpose of prostitution.

(B) MEANING OF TERMS
■ 1. 'That you'
Means the identity of the person loitering or soliciting.
■ 2. 'being a common prostitute'
'Common prostitute' means only female and does not include male prostitutes (*DPP v Bull* [1994] 4 All ER 411). Prostitution is not confined to sexual intercourse. A woman who offers her body commonly for any lewd act for reward is a common prostitute. This includes a woman who merely masturbates her clients (*R v Webb* [1964] 1 QB 357). Before being charged with being a common prostitute, loitering or soliciting etc, the police should first caution the woman on two occasions for loitering or soliciting etc. The caution should be entered in the appropriate register of cautions. A detailed description of the woman and all other means of identifying the woman in the future should be noted as prostitutes frequently change their names and appearances.
■ 3. 'did loiter (or solicit)'
'Loiter' means passing frequently at a slow speed (*Williamson v Wright* 1924 SLT 363). Solicit means to invite, entice, appeal to, or request another person. An advertisement or notice board is not soliciting as the presence of the prostitute is required (*Burge v Director of Public Prosecutions* [1962] 1 All ER 666 and *Weisz v Monahan* [1962] 1 All ER 694). A person who is in a street or public place can be solicited by a prostitute who is on a balcony or at a window (*Smith v Hughes* [1960] 2 All ER 859).
■ 4. 'in a street (or public place) called ....'
'Street' is defined at section 1(4) Street Offences Act 1959 as any bridge, road, lane, footway, subway, square, court, alley or passage, whether a thoroughfare or not, which is for the time being open to the public, and the doorways and entrances of premises abutting on a street and any ground adjoining and open to a street, shall form part of the street.

'Public place' has been held to include a field used by the public on one day only; a racecourse enclosure where there was a right to exclude people and charge for admission; and an inn car park. The cases concerned are *R v Collinson* (1931) 23 Cr App R 49, *Glynn v Simmonds* [1952] 2 All ER 47 and *Elkins v Cartlidge* [1947] 1 All ER 829 respectively.

■ **5. 'for the purpose of prostitution'.**
Means that loitering or soliciting must be for the purpose of offering her body etc, for reward as outlined at point 2 above.

(C) USUAL METHODS OF PROVING THESE POINTS
■ **1. 'That you'**
This point can be proved by the police officer who arrested (or occasionally reports) the prostitute, identifying her to the court.

■ **2. 'being a common prostitute'**
Proof of this point must be available to negate any defence of accident or mistake, eg, 'That I was waiting for my boy friend or taxi etc.' The proof usually takes the form of quoting previous convictions, cautions and other relevant antecedent history to the court, where she denies on oath being a common prostitute. The officer(s) who actually cautioned her may be required to prove such caution(s) to the court.

■ **3. 'did loiter (or solicit)'**
Two police officers will keep observations for prostitutes and to prove this point their evidence should contain words to the effect that, 'the accused walked slowly up and down High Street five times, stopping and talking to several men. As a result of what one of the men (the witness) John Smith said to me I spoke to the accused etc'. Here the prostitute both loiters and eventually solicits when she speaks to a client. Proof of soliciting is the actual conversational meeting with a prospective client. Usually in practice only one of the charges is preferred, ie loitering (over a period of time) or soliciting (usually a verbal invitation).

■ **4. 'in a street (or public place)'**
This point is proved by naming the street and in nine times out

of 10 will cause no problems. But in cases of doubt the definition at point (B)4 should be consulted and the particular place proved by describing how the place comes within the definition.

■ **5. 'for the purpose of prostitution'.**

This point must be carefully proved to eliminate any risk of charging an innocent woman who was merely asking the way or for a light etc. Good evidence would consist of an incriminating statement taken from a prospective client or an offer to do 'business' with a plain-clothed policeman.

10A. KERB CRAWLING
Section 1 Sexual Offences Act 1985

(A) POINTS TO PROVE
1. That you (a man) 2. did solicit a woman (or different women) 3. for the purpose of prostitution 4. from a motor vehicle 5. while in a street or public place.
6. persistently or in a manner likely to cause annoyance to the women solicited (or nuisance to others in the neighbourhood).

(B) MEANING OF TERMS
■ **1. 'That you (a man)'**

Means the identity of the kerb crawler. The word 'man' also includes 'boy'.

■ **2. 'did solicit a woman (or different women)'**

'Solicit means to invite, entice, appeal to or request a woman. It has been held that to drive a car at night again and again along a street used by prostitutes did not amount to 'soliciting'. There must be a physical act or words amounting to solicitation, *Darroch v DPP* [1990] Crim LR 814. The word 'woman' also includes 'girl'. The woman could be an innocent pedestrian or a prostitute.

■ **3. 'for the purpose of prostitution'**
Prostitution is defined at (B)2 of the previous offence 10 and 'soliciting for prostitution' in this Act means soliciting her for the purpose of obtaining her services as a prostitute.

■ **4. 'from a motor vehicle'**
'Motor vehicle' has the same meaning as in the Road Traffic Act (see Glossary). Normally it will be from a car or small van.

■ **5. 'while in a street or public place'**
'Street' and public place are defined at (B)4 of offence 10. No offence is committed under this section if it takes place in private.

■ **6. 'persistently or in a manner likely to cause annoyance to the woman solicited (or nuisance to others in the neighbourhood)'.**
This point is not defined and it is considered that soliciting one woman on one occasion would not amount to this offence. The soliciting of at least two women on the same occasion or one woman on more than one occasion may be sufficient. It is also considered that the likely nuisance would be of a general type within the area and there would be no requirement to prove a nuisance to a particular person.

(C) USUAL METHODS OF PROVING THESE POINTS
■ **1. 'That you (a man)'**
This can be proved in a statement from the female concerned or other witness(es), including the officer in the case.

■ **2. 'did solicit a woman'**
Evidence from the woman or other witness(es) to show an invitation/enticement /request etc is necessary. For example, for the man to say to the woman: 'Are you doing business?' or 'How much do you charge?'

■ **3. 'for the purpose of prostitution'**
This is proved by what the man said or intended. It is his state of mind and may be best proved by question and answer in the police interview or by what he said to the victim.

■ **4. 'from a motor vehicle'**

The vehicle should be described in the witness statement(s) and backed up by the accused's admissions in the police interview.

■ **5. 'while in a street or public place'**

Again the witness(s) would describe the venue in their statements to prove this point, as the essence of this offence is its public nuisance element.

■ **6. 'persistently or in a manner likely to cause annoyance to the woman solicited (or nuisance to others in the neighbourhood)'.**

This point would be best proved by taking statements from the women or woman concerned to show 'persistency', 'likely annoyance' or 'nuisance.'

Besides the prosecution proving annoyance or nuisance the magistrates can take account of their local knowledge of the regular presence of prostitutes in a particular area and of the fact that an area is heavily populated, *Paul v DPP* (1989) 153 JP 512, DC.

11. TAKING CONVEYANCE WITHOUT AUTHORITY
Section 12(1) Theft Act 1968

(A) POINTS TO PROVE
1. That you 2. did, without having the consent of the owner or other lawful authority, 3. take a certain conveyance, namely a .... 4. for your own use (or for the use of ....).

(B) MEANING OF TERMS
■ **1. 'That you'**

Means the identity of the person taking the conveyance.

■ 2. 'did, without having the consent of the owner or other lawful authority'

Means that this offence is not committed if the accused believed that he had lawful authority to do it or that he would have had the owner's consent if the owner knew of his doing it and the circumstances of it. In practice this defence is not often put forward. 'Other lawful authority' includes such things as the police moving a vehicle causing an obstruction.

'Owner' includes a person possessing the conveyance as a result of a hiring agreement or a hire-purchase agreement.

■ 3. 'take a certain conveyance, namely a ....'

'Take' means some movement of the conveyance intending to put the conveyance into motion (*Blayney v Knight* [1975] Crim LR 237). 'Conveyance' means any conveyance construed or adapted for the carriage of a person or persons whether by land, water or air, except that it does not include a conveyance constructed or adapted for use only under the control of a person not carried in or on it, and 'drive' shall be construed accordingly. As the essence of this offence is stealing a ride, handcarts and pedestrian-controlled vehicles etc, are not conveyances as they are designed for use only under the control of a person not carried in or on it. Pedal cycles are not included under section 12(1) but are specially dealt with under section 12(5).

■ 4. 'for your own use (or for the use of ....)'.

Means that a 'use' must be obtained. For example where the handbrake of a motor car is released and the car is allowed to run down a hill by itself the offence under section 12 would not be committed as it was not for his or another's use.

(C) USUAL METHODS OF PROVING THESE POINTS
■ 1. 'That you'

Is normally proved by the officer who saw the defendant driving etc, or another witness who can swear the defendant was driving etc, or by the defendant's admission.

■ **2. 'did without having the consent of the owner or other lawful authority'**

When the complainant's statement is obtained it should include the point that the person concerned had not got his (the owner's) consent to take the conveyance.

■ **3. 'take a certain conveyance namely a ....'**

In the majority of cases the conveyance will be a motor car and the 'taking' is proved by a witness stating that he saw the defendant take the car, or by an admission to that effect by the defendant. Only the slightest movement need be proved but in practice the car will probably have travelled several miles.

'Conveyance' can be proved by describing the thing concerned and in cases of difficulty by showing that it comes within the definition of a conveyance as shown as (B)(3) of this offence.

■ **4. 'for your own use (or for the use of ....)'.**

The normal 'use' is to go for a joyride, to get home after missing the last bus or train or for use in crime. The fact that it was used for his or another's use could be established by questions and answers between the police and the defendant.

(D) SUPPORTING EVIDENCE

Note 1. A consent obtained by a false statement as to the destination or the purpose of the journey is still valid (*R v Peart* [1970] 2 All ER 823).

Note 2. The second half of section 12(1) deals with a person who, knowing that a conveyance has been taken without authority, drives it or allows himself to be carried in or on it.

Note 3. See also offence 30, interference with a motor vehicle or trailers or with anything carried in or o a motor vehicle or trailer (section 9 Criminal Attempts Act 1981).

Note 4. Also consider 'aggravated vehicle-taking' section12A Theft Act 1968 (as inserted by the Aggravated Vehicle-Taking Act 1992) viz: commits an offence contrary to section 12(1) above re a mechanically propelled vehicle, and at any time after the taking:

(a) the vehicle is driven dangerously on a road/public place;

(b) an 'injury accident' occurred owing to the driving of the vehicle;

(c) a 'damage or property accident' occurs owing to the driving of that vehicle;

(d) damage is caused to the taken vehicle (including damage caused by the defendant trying to escape from the vehicle (*Dawes v DPP* [1994] RTR 209)).

Aggravated vehicle-taking attracts an increased penalty. Defences include that the damage/accident/driving took place before the taking or when the defendant was not in or on, or in the immediate vicinity of, the taken vehicle.

12. BURGLARY - COMMITTING THEFT HAVING ENTERED
Section 9(1) (b) Theft Act 1968

(A) POINTS TO PROVE
1. That you 2. did, having entered 3. a certain building (or part of a certain building) namely .... 4. as a trespasser, 5. did steal therein (specify) ....

(B) MEANING OF TERMS
■ **1. 'That you'**
Means the identity of the burglar.
■ **2. 'did, having entered'**
Means that an effective and substantial entry has been made (*R v Collins* [1972] 2 All ER 1105). An entry can be made by any part of the accused's body or by an instrument held by the accused to intimidate someone in the building or to remove

goods from the building. An entry cannot be made by an instrument used to make an entry such as a key or piece of wire used to pull back internal bolts. It is submitted that whether or not an entry has been made is a question of fact for the jury to decide.

■ 3. 'a certain building (or part of a certain building) namely ....'

'Building' means a substantial, permanent structure, usually constructed of brick, stone or wood, or any combination of them, which has walls and a roof. Again, this issue is one of fact for the jury, not one of law. Inhabited vehicles or vessels are included, eg houseboats or caravans, even if the inhabitant is not there (section 9(3) Theft Act 1968).

'Part of a building' will include entering a building lawfully but then going into a part of the building as a trespasser, such as entering the private quarters in a public house which was entered lawfully in the first instance or going behind an unattended counter in a shop.

■ 4. 'as a trespasser'

Means an intentional entry, whether reckless or negligent, into a building which is in possession of another who does not consent to the entry. The accused must know he is a trespasser or be reckless to that fact. Bogus officials, who gain entry fraudulently, would still be trespassers.

■ 5. 'did steal therein (specify) ....'.

Means steal anything contrary to sections 1 to 6 of the Theft Act 1968, see offence 13.

(C) USUAL METHODS OF PROVING THESE POINTS

■ 1. 'That you'

Apart from being caught in the act, when the burglar may be identified by the witness concerned, forensic evidence sometimes helps to prove identity. Fingerprints, fibres of clothing, footprints or gloveprints etc, could be used where appropriate.

■ 2. 'did, having entered'

In the majority of burglaries this point should not be difficult to prove and a line in a witness statement to the effect, 'I saw James Stewart enter the house', would suffice. In the case of instruments, proof of the accused's intent when entering the building with the instrument would be required, ie was the instrument only used to gain entry (no entry) or was it used to intimidate or to steal goods? (When there would be an entry.)

■ 3. 'a certain building (or part of a certain building) namely ....'

A description of the building concerned in a witness statement would be sufficient proof of this point. Generally burglaries involve dwelling houses, warehouses, schools, shops etc.

■ 4. 'as a trespasser'

A sentence in the complainant's statement such as, 'This is my house and James had no right or authority to enter', is normally sufficient.

■ 5. 'did steal therein (specify) ....'.

A theft must be proved. (See offence 13 of this section for such advice.)

(D) SUPPORTING EVIDENCE

Note 1. Attempt to steal can also be charged, as can inflicting or attempting to inflict grievous bodily harm (GBH) on any person therein.

Note 2. The offence at section 9(1)(a) of the Theft Act 1968 can be charged where a person enters a building or part of a building as a trespasser with intent to commit theft, GBH, rape or unlawful damage.

Note 3. Aggravated burglary can be charged when a section 9 burglary has been committed and the accused has with him/her any firearm, imitation firearm, any weapon of offence or any explosive. This offence carries life imprisonment.

13. THEFT
Sections 1 to 7 Theft Act 1968

(A) POINTS TO PROVE
1. That you 2. did steal .... (specify property) of the value of .... 3. the property of ....

(B) MEANING OF TERMS
■ 1. 'That you'
Means the identity of the person who stole the property.
■ 2. 'did steal .... (specify property) of the value of ....'
'Steal' means (i) dishonestly (ii) appropriates (iii) property (iv) belonging to another (v) with the intention of permanently depriving the other of it.

(i) 'Dishonestly' generally means without a claim of right made in good faith. It will not be dishonest where the accused believes he had a right in law to the property or that he would have had the other's consent to take the property.

(ii) 'Appropriates' means any assumption of the rights of an owner and includes coming by property without stealing it but later assuming the rights of ownership. For example, a boy under 10 years, the age of criminal responsibility, took his friend's bicycle home and gave it to his father. Although the father came by the bicycle innocently, if he assumes the rights of an owner by selling it, for instance, he will steal it.

(iii) 'Property' - what is stolen must come within the definition of property viz: money and all other property, real or personal, including things in action and other intangible property. There are exceptions to this definition concerning land, mushrooms, wild plants and wild creatures.

(iv) 'Belonging to another' briefly means belonging to someone having possession or control of the property. Possession includes a constructive possession as well as actual possession.

A person can have possession or control of property without knowing of its existence (*R v Woodman* [1974] 2 All ER 955).

(v) 'With the intention of permanently depriving the other of it' briefly means treating the property as his own regardless of the other's rights, eg giving the property away, selling it or painting it, etc. An intent to deprive temporarily is not sufficient.

■ **3. 'the property of ....'.**
Means as point 2(iv) above, the person having possession or control of the property,

(C) USUAL METHODS OF PROVING THESE POINTS
■ **1. 'That you'**
Is usually proved by someone witnessing the theft, but can be proved by fingerprints, an admission by the accused, being found in possession of the stolen property, and by the use of a variety of technical aids such as a concealed camera.

■ **2. 'did steal ....'**
Proof of the five parts of stealing will be dealt with as follows: (i) dishonestly (ii) appropriates (iii) property (iv) belonging to another (v) with the intention of permanently depriving the other of it.

(i) 'Dishonestly' is proved by the person to whom the property belonged stating that, 'No person had any right or authority to take the property'.

(ii) 'Appropriates' is generally proved by a witness stating that the accused picked the property up or put it in a shopping bag or a pocket. If the accused was not seen to take the property such evidence as him being seen near the scene of the crime or being found in possession of the property is useful. As appropriates involves assuming the rights of an owner the interview between the police officer in the case and the accused can be important. It can help to show his motive or state of mind if carefully worded questions are put to the accused.

(iii) 'Property' is proved in most cases by describing it in the statement of the person to whom it belongs or in the police officer's statement. In most cases it will be personal, or in other words movable, property.

(iv) 'Belonging to another' is proved by showing that the property was appropriated from someone having possession or control of it, eg the owner or tenant etc, of a dwelling house would have possession and control of all the personal property in the house, and the owner or driver of a car would have possession or control of the contents of the car. A sentence in the loser's statement to the effect that, 'the last time I saw my watch was when I put it in my locker at work' or, 'I placed my purse in my shopping basket' shows that he had possession or control of the property,

(v) 'With the intention of permanently depriving the other of it'. In order to prove this intent it must be shown that the accused meant to treat the property as his own.

In practice the following examples would probably show this intent:

(a) a shoplifter placing goods in his pocket or shopping bag where wire baskets are provided. It is safer and more conclusive to let the shoplifter pass through any checkout without paying;

(b) a burglar leaving premises with property;

(c) a car thief who alters registration plates or the colour; or

(d) a pickpocket running off with the victim's wallet;

(e) a council tenant had removed council doors and replaced them with his own - it was held that he had treated the council doors as his own regardless of the council's rights (*DPP v Lavender* [1994] Crim LR 297).

The accused's intentions are best proved from any admission he makes when interviewed by the police.

■ 3. 'the property of ....'.
This point is proved as at 2(iv) above.

(D) SUPPORTING EVIDENCE

Where a person is found in possession of recently stolen property it can be presumed by the court that he stole it, in the absence of a satisfactory explanation.

14. OBTAINING PROPERTY BY DECEPTION
Section 15 Theft Act 1968

(A) POINTS TO PROVE
1. That you 2. did, by a certain deception, namely ....
3. dishonestly 4. obtain 5. certain property, namely ....
6. belonging to .... (specify person) 7. with the intention of permanently depriving .... of the said property.

(B) MEANING OF TERMS
■ 1. 'That you'
Means the identity of the person committing the offence.
■ 2. 'did, by a certain deception, namely ....'
'Deception' means any deception (whether deliberate or reckless) by words or conduct as to fact or as to law, including a deception as to the present intentions of the person using the deception or any other person. It was held to be a deception where a deliberate misrepresentation for housing benefit was made as the housing authority needed to know the truth before paying it (*R v Talbott* [1995] Crim LR 396 CA). A deliberate deception would include an outright untruth and a reckless deception would include a case where the deceiver makes a statement and is indifferent to its being true or false. The deception must operate on the mind of the person from whom the property was obtained. In other words, if property is obtained

because the intended victim takes pity on the accused and not because of the deception, then property has not been obtained 'by a certain deception'.

■ 3. 'dishonestly'

'Dishonestly' is not defined and section 2(1) of the Theft Act 1968 does not apply to section 15. However, the obtaining must be dishonest. Therefore, if the accused uses a deception to obtain property to which he feels he is entitled, he will not 'obtain dishonestly'. Whether or not dishonesty is present is a question for the court to decide. In *R v Ghosh* [1982] 2All ER 689 a more general definition of 'dishonesty' was given, ie the court must decide whether:

(a) what was done was dishonest according to the ordinary standards of reasonable and honest people, AND

(b) if so, did the defendant himself, realise that his actions were, according to those standards, dishonest?

■ 4. 'obtained'

Is defined in section 15(2) as follows: For the purposes of this section a person is to be treated as obtaining property if he obtains ownership, possession or control of it, and 'obtain' includes obtaining for another or enabling another to obtain or to retain.

'Ownership' is obtained when the accused gets the best title to the property and the previous owner relinquishes any claim to the property. 'Possession' is obtained when the accused gets physical possession of the property and this can be done without affecting the ownership in any way. 'Control' is wider in meaning than 'possession' and the accused could be in control of property without owning or being in physical possession of the said property.

■ 5. 'certain property namely ....'

'Property' is defined at section 4(1) of the Theft Act 1968 and is at (B)2(iii) of offence 13, theft. Note that the exceptions to the definition of property concerning theft of land and certain plants and animals do not apply to section 15.

■ 6. 'belonging to .... (specify person)'
Means, briefly, that it must belong to someone having possession or control of the property. See (B)2(iv) of offence 13, theft.

■ **7. 'with the intention of permanently depriving .... of the said property'.**
Means, briefly, treating the property as his own regardless of the other's rights, such as, selling, intentionally damaging or giving away the property.

(C) USUAL METHODS OF PROVING THESE POINTS

■ 1. 'That you'
Is usually proved by the person to whom the property belonged stating that it was the accused who deceived him.

■ **2. 'did, by a certain deception'**
This point is normally proved by the person deceived, describing the deception in his statement and pointing out that it was as a result of the deception that he parted with the property to the accused.

■ **3. 'dishonestly'**
'Dishonestly' can be proved by the victim stating that the accused had no right to the property or the accused stating that he had no right or claim to the property.

■ **4. 'obtained'**
In most cases the accused obtains physical possession and ownership of the property because of the deception and this can usually be proved by the victim eg, 'As a result of the deception I gave him (the accused) five pounds'.

■ **5. 'certain property, namely ....'**
'Property can be proved by the victim describing the article in question and the police officer ensuring that it comes within the definition of property at (B)5 of this offence.

■ **6. 'belonging to .... (specify person)'**
Is proved as at (C)2(iv) of offence 13, theft. A sentence in the victim's statement to the effect that, 'This was my property

..........' or 'I was left in control of the property ....' or 'I had the library book in my possession etc', would prove this point.

■ **7. 'With the intention of permanently depriving .... of the said property'.**

See (C)2(v) of offence 13, theft, for the proof of this point.

15. HANDLING STOLEN GOODS
Section 22 Theft Act 1968

(A) POINTS TO PROVE
1. That you, 2. knowing (or believing) 3. certain stolen goods namely .... to be stolen 4. did dishonestly 5. receive them.

(B) MEANING OF TERMS
■ **1. 'That you'**

Means the identity of the person receiving the stolen goods.

■ **2. 'knowing (or believing)'**

The prosecution must prove that the accused 'knew' or at least 'believed' that the goods were stolen at the time of receiving them.

■ **3. 'certain stolen goods namely .... to be stolen'**

Means that the prosecution must prove that the goods were still stolen at the time they were received. For example, they would cease to be stolen where the goods had been discovered by the police who had taken control of them and were watching for the handler coming to collect them, or where the owner had ceased to have any right of restitution to the goods.

'Stolen goods' are defined in section 24 of the Theft Act 1968 as:

(1) The provisions of this Act relating to goods which have been stolen shall apply whether the stealing occurred in England or Wales or elsewhere, and whether it occurred before or after the commencement of this Act - provided that the stealing (if not an offence under this Act) amounted to an offence where,

and at the time when, the goods were stolen - and references to stolen goods shall be construed accordingly.

(2) For purposes of these provisions, references to stolen goods shall include - in addition to the goods originally stolen and parts of them (whether in their original state or not) - (a) any other goods which directly or indirectly represent or have at any time represented the stolen goods in the hands of the thief as being the proceeds of any disposal or realisation of the whole or part of the goods stolen or of goods so representing the stolen goods; and (b) any other goods which directly or indirectly represent or have at any time represented the stolen goods in the hands of a handler of the stolen goods or any part of them as being the proceeds of any disposal or realisation of the whole or part of the stolen goods handled by him or of goods so representing them.

(3) But no goods shall be regarded as having continued to be stolen goods after they have been restored to the person from whom they were stolen or to other lawful possession or custody, or after that person and any other person claiming through him have otherwise ceased as regards those goods to have any right to restitution in respect of the theft.

(4) For purposes of the provisions of this Act relating to goods which have been stolen (including subsections (1) to (3) above) goods obtained in England or Wales or elsewhere either by blackmail or in the circumstances described in section 15(1) of this Act shall be regarded as stolen and 'steal', 'theft' and 'thief' shall be construed accordingly.

Note 1. The phrase 'in the hands of the thief' as used in subsection 2(a) above means in the possession or under the control of the thief, *R v Forsyth* [1997] 2 Crim App Rep 299 CA.
Note 2. 'Restored' as used in subsection (3) means taken into possession and not merely kept under observation (Attorney-General's Reference (No 1 of 1974) [1974] 2 All ER 899).

■ 4. 'did dishonestly'

'Dishonesty' is defined at (B)2(i) of offence 13, theft. Under the old Larceny Act of 1916 it was said that dishonesty was 'fraudulently and without a claim of right made in good faith'.

■ 5. 'receive them'.

'Receiving' means acquiring exclusive control over the stolen goods or a joint possession with the thief or handler. There are numerous circumstances in which a person can 'handle' stolen goods but 'receiving' is the most common type. The other ways include 'undertaking or assisting in the retention, removal, disposal or realisation by or for the benefit of another or arranging to do so etc.'

(C) USUAL METHODS OF PROVING THESE POINTS

■ 1. 'That you'

The actual receiving will usually take place without being witnessed, therefore proving the accused's identity is usually on his admission and occasionally is similar to some thefts, ie proving identity by a concealed camera or photograph.

■ 2. 'knowing (or believing)

This knowledge, which is sometimes called 'guilty knowledge', is proved by the admission of the accused, by circumstantial evidence or by 'special evidence'. Circumstantial evidence could consist of altering or destroying identification marks; carefully concealing the stolen property; purchase at a lower price than the goods are worth; or failing to keep records where necessary, such as a scrap metal dealer.

Special evidence is dealt with at section 27(3) of the Theft Act 1968 as follows: Where a person is being proceeded against for handling stolen goods (but not for any offence other than handling stolen goods) then at any stage of the proceedings, if evidence has been given of his having or arranging to have in his possession the goods the subject of the charge, or of his undertaking or assisting in or arranging to undertake or assist in, their retention, removal, disposal or realisation, the following evidence shall be admissible for the purpose of proving that he knew or believed the goods to be stolen goods:

(a) evidence that he has had in his possession, or has undertaken or assisted in the retention, removal, disposal or realisation of, stolen goods from any theft taking place not earlier than 12 months before the offence charged: and

(b) (provided that seven days' notice in writing has been given to him of the intention to prove the conviction) evidence that he has within the five years preceding the date of the offence charged been convicted of theft or of handling stolen goods.

Therefore this provision allows the prosecution to bring the accused's more recent previous activities and convictions before the court.

The difficulties of proving what a person 'knows' or 'believes' also attracted common law assistance. Evidence of a thief that he had previously sold stolen property to the accused is admissible. Where the suspected 'handler' is found in possession of recently stolen property the court can presume that he stole or 'knowingly' received the goods if the accused does not provide an explanation of his possession or his explanation is unsatisfactory. It is for the prosecution to establish these facts, but they can be rebutted by the defence.

The following guidelines were given by the Court of Appeal with regard to proving 'knowing or believing' (*R v Hall* (1985) 81 Cr App Rep 260). 'Knowing' is for example when the accused is told that goods are stolen by someone with first hand knowledge, possibly the thief or burglar. 'Belief' is not quite 'knowledge' and could be said to be the state of mind of the accused who says to himself or herself: 'I cannot say I know for certain that these are stolen goods, but there can be no other reasonable conclusion in the light of all the circumstances, and in the light of all that I have seen and heard.' Where either of these states of mind can be proved then 'knowing or believing' can be established.

■ **3. 'certain stolen goods namely .... to be stolen'**

This point can be proved by taking a statement from the owner of the stolen goods in which he states the details of the theft. The prosecution must go further than this and prove that the goods were still stolen at the time of the handling. Points should be mentioned such as, no one had taken lawful possession or control of the goods; that they had not been returned to the owner; or that the owner had not ceased to have rights of restitution to the goods AND that the goods were still stolen goods.

■ **4. 'did dishonestly'**

Dishonesty can be proved by showing the handler had no claim of right to the stolen goods or that the owner had not given the accused any authority to handle the stolen goods etc.

■ **5. 'receive them'.**

This point can be proved by showing the accused acquired exclusive control or a joint possession of the stolen goods. The most usual way this point is proved is to show that the accused had physical possession of the stolen goods.

16. CRIMINAL DAMAGE
Section 1(1) Criminal Damage Act 1971

(A) POINTS TO PROVE

1. That you 2. without lawful excuse 3. destroyed (or damaged) .... (specify property) 4. belonging to .... (specify person) 5. intending to destroy or damage) such property or being reckless as to whether such property would be destroyed (or damaged).

(B) MEANING OF TERMS

■ **1. 'That you'**

Means the identity of the accused.

■ 2. 'without lawful excuse'

Is defined at section 5 of the Criminal Damage Act 1971:

(1) This section applies to any offence under section 1(1) and any offence under sections 2 or 3 other than one involving a threat by the person charged to destroy or damage property in a way which he knows is likely to endanger the life of another or involving an intent by the person charged to use or cause or permit the use of something in his custody or under his control so to destroy or damage property.

(2) A person charged with an offence to which this section applies shall, whether or not he would be treated for the purposes of this Act as having a lawful excuse apart from this subsection, be treated for those purposes as having a lawful excuse:

   (a) if at the time of the act or acts alleged to constitute the offence he believed that the person or persons whom he believed to be entitled to consent to the destruction of or damage to the property in question had so consented, or would have so consented to it if he or they had known of the destruction or damage and its circumstances; or

   (b) if he destroyed or damaged or threatened to destroy or damage the property in question or, in the case of a charge of an offence under section 3, intended to use or cause or permit the use of something to destroy or damage it, in order to protect property belonging to himself or another or a right or interest in property which was or which he believed to be vested in himself or another, and at the time of the act or acts alleged to constitute the offence he believed -

     (i) that the property, right or interest was in immediate need of protection; and

     (ii) that the means of protection adopted or proposed to be adopted were or would be reasonable having regard to all the circumstances.

Note this excuse is limited to the offences under the Criminal Damage Act which do not involve danger to life. It is also worthy of note that the accused must honestly believe in his actions under this proviso. In *Lloyd v DPP* [1992] 1 All ER 982, it was held that a person did not have a 'lawful excuse' when he damaged a wheel clamp on his car after parking unlawfully in a private car park.

■ **3. 'destroyed (or damaged) .... (specify property)'**
'Destroyed' means that the property is totally ruined or permanently spoilt. 'Damaged' means something less permanent than destroyed, eg where property can be repaired or has only been partly damaged so as to reduce its value or usefulness.

'Property' is defined by section 10 of the Criminal Damage Act 1971 as: (1) In this Act 'property means property of a tangible nature, whether real or personal, including money and –

(a) including wild creatures which have been tamed or are ordinarily kept in captivity, and any other wild creature or their carcasses if, but only if, they have been reduced into possession which has not been lost or abandoned or are in the course of being reduced into possession; but

(b) not including mushrooms growing wild on any land or flowers, fruit or foliage of a plant growing wild on any land.

For the purposes of this subsection 'mushroom' includes any fungus and 'plant' includes any shrub or tree. The main differences between this definition of property and the one in the Theft Act is that the Criminal Damage Act definition does not include intangible property, but does include land. A computer 'hacker' can be convicted of criminal damage after obtaining unauthorised entry to a computer system and making alterations impairing its proper use, *R v Whiteley* [1991] Crim LR 436.

■ **4. 'belonging to .... (specify person)'**
'Belonging to' means briefly per section 10(2) of the Criminal

Damage Act 1971, any person who has: (a) custody or control of; (b) any proprietary right or interest in; or (c) a charge on, the property in question. Generally, 'custody or control' as at (a) ante will cater for most offences of criminal damage.

■ **5. 'intending to destroy (or damage) such property or being reckless as to whether such property would be destroyed (or damaged)'.**

'Intending' means an actual wish, desire or aim to do the damage that was done. 'Reckless' means having foresight of the natural and probable consequences of his acts or carrying out a deliberate act when closing his mind to the obvious risk of damage to the property.

(C) USUAL METHODS OF PROVING THESE POINTS

■ **1. 'That you'**

Is normally proved by someone witnessing the damage or admission by the accused during questioning by the police.

■ **2. 'without lawful excuse'**

It is for the defendant to put forward any lawful excuse during the investigation of the suspected offence. It is then for the prosecution to disprove any lawful excuse which could provide a defence under section 5 of the Criminal Damage Act 1971 (see (B)2). Where no excuse is put forward it is usual practice to include in the victim's statement words to the effect, 'No person had any right or authority to damage the property'.

■ **3. 'destroyed (or damaged) .... (specify property)'**

This point can be proved by describing the extent of the damage or destruction in the statement of the victim or some other witness. Where there is any doubt as to whether property has been destroyed (ie totally ruined) the easier charge to prove would be 'damaged', ie mere partial damage is sufficient. 'Property' is proved by describing the article concerned in one of the above statements and ensuring it falls within the definition at (B)3 of this offence.

■ **4. 'belonging to .... (specify person)'**

In most cases of damage this point is proved by the owner of the property stating that, 'This is my property .... etc.'

■ **5. 'intending to destroy (or damage) such property or being reckless as to whether such property would be destroyed (or damaged)'.**

This point shows that the prosecution must prove that the accused had either an intention to destroy or damage etc, or was at least reckless as to whether the property was destroyed or damaged. When proving a person's intentions or foresight, section 8 of the Criminal Justice Act 1967 provides: A court or jury, in determining whether a person has committed an offence -

(a) shall not be bound in law to infer that he intended or foresaw a result of his actions by reason only of its being a natural and probable consequence of those actions; but

(b) shall decide whether he did intend or foresee that result by reference to all the evidence, drawing such inferences from the evidence as appear proper in the circumstances.

Therefore such intent or foresight is usually proved by questions and answers to the effect, 'Did you realise that your actions would result in the damage you have caused?' Where the answer is, 'Yes' the case is straightforward. Where, 'No' is given, then the questioning should try to elicit that the accused was a reasonably educated person who should have realised or foreseen the consequences of his actions.

Note that the court will look at all the evidence available, not just what the accused says, before drawing any inferences. The Law Commission (Law Comm No 89) recommended the following test for recklessness: Did the person whose conduct is in issue foresee that his conduct might produce the result; AND if so, was it unreasonable for him to take the risk of producing it?

Therefore, to prove recklessness, the prosecution may ask the accused questions like, 'Did you foresee the result of your conduct ....?' Where the answer is, 'Yes' the questioning could continue, 'If you foresaw the result why did you take the risk of producing it?' Where the answer shows that the accused's actions were 'unreasonable' then 'recklessness' will probably be proved.

(D) SUPPORTING EVIDENCE

Note 1. The charge should include whether the value of the damage is over or under £5,000 or whether the value is unknown. This affects the mode of trial and penalty. Where a previously unknown amount is later determined, the charge should be amended accordingly.

Note 2. The consent of the DPP is required where the damage is to the accused spouse's property.

17. TRESPASSING WITH A FIREARM
Section 20(2) Firearms Act 1968

(A) POINTS TO PROVE
1. That you 2. while you had a certain firearm, namely .... 3. with you 4. did enter (or were) on certain land situated at .... 5. as a trespasser and without reasonable excuse.

(B) MEANING OF TERMS
■ 1. 'That you'
Means the identity of the accused.
■ 2. 'while you had a certain firearm, namely a ....'
'Firearm' is defined at section 57(1) of the Firearms Act 1968 as: In this Act, the expression 'firearm' means a lethal barrelled weapon of any description from which any shot, bullet or other missile can be discharged and includes -
(a) any prohibited weapon, whether it is such a lethal weapon as aforesaid or not;

(b) any component part of such a lethal or prohibited weapon;

(c) any accessory to any such weapon designed or adapted to diminish the noise or flash caused by firing the weapon;

and so much of section 1 of this Act as excludes any description of firearms from the category of firearms to which that section applies shall be construed as also excluding component parts of, and accessories to, firearms of that description.

■ 3. 'with you'

This point means a close physical link with immediate control over the firearm. However, it is not necessary to prove that the accused had actually been carrying the firearm (*R v Kelt* [1977] 3 All ER 1099). Therefore where a car driver has a firearm on the passenger seat at the side of him it could be said to be 'with him'.

■ 4. 'did enter (or were) on certain land situated at ....'

'Enter' or 'were on' cover the occasions when it can be proved that the accused entered land or where he was on the land. 'Land' includes land covered by water or in other words lakes, rivers, ponds etc.

■ 5. 'as a trespasser and without reasonable excuse'.

'Trespasser' means that he had no licence or permission to enter or be on the land. 'Without reasonable excuse' means that the accused has not put forward an excuse for entering or being on the land which amounts to a reasonable excuse. Examples of excuses that the courts could accept as reasonable include: entering on land accidentally on a foggy day or night; entering to save life or property or being on land because of a mistake regarding permission or the location of the land.

(C) USUAL METHODS OF PROVING THESE POINTS

■ 1. 'That you'

Could be proved by the witness who saw the defendant identifying him or on the defendant's admission.

■ 2. 'while you had a certain firearm, namely a .... '

■ 3. 'with you'

Again, in the vast majority of cases there will be no doubt the defendant has the firearm 'with him' and the point can be proved by a witness stating that the defendant was carrying the firearm. In more difficult cases the prosecution must prove that there was a close physical link between the firearm and the defendant and that he had immediate control over it.

■ **4. 'did enter (or were) on certain land situated at ....'**
This point can be established by a witness describing how he saw the defendant enter on to land or that he was present on the land. 'Land' can be proved by a witness describing the land or land covered by water eg, 'I saw him in the middle of my three acre field' or, 'I saw him in the middle of my private fishing lake in an inflatable dinghy'.

■ **5. 'as a trespasser and without reasonable excuse'.**
This point can be proved by obtaining a statement from the owner or person responsible for the land in question to the effect that the defendant did not have any right or authority to enter or be on the land. Any 'reasonable excuse' put forward by the defendant which appears to be untrue or suspicious, should be tested by making enquiries to verify the truth and putting questions to the defendant, which can then be recorded in the police officer's statement of evidence.

18. GOING EQUIPPED FOR BURGLARY, THEFT OR CHEAT
Section 25(1) Theft Act 1968

(A) POINTS TO PROVE
1. That you 2. not being at your place of abode, namely at .... 3. had with you 4. a certain article namely a .... (briefly describe article) for use in the course of (or in connection with) burglary (or theft) (or cheat).

(B) MEANING OF TERMS
■ 1. 'That you'
Means the identity of the person 'going equipped'.
■ 2. 'not being at your place of abode, namely at ....'
Means being elsewhere than where he lived. Usually such offences are detected by searching suspect vehicles and persons late at night.
■ 3. 'had with you'
Means actually had with him as opposed to any constructive possession, such as keeping a set of skeleton keys some miles away from where he worked for the purpose of opening car doors.
■ 4. 'a certain article namely a ....'.
This point means any article which was made or adapted for use relating to 'burglary', 'theft' or 'cheat'. Examples include skeleton keys (made), marked playing cards (adapted) or a printed card stating falsely that the holder is collecting for Oxfam. It also means anything, even if not made or adapted, which the defendant had with him for use in the course of burglary etc, eg screwdriver, brace and bit, jemmy, gloves and car keys.

Taking a conveyance is included in 'theft' and obtaining by deception in 'cheat', for example a vendor selling counterfeit goods.

(C) USUAL METHODS OF PROVING THESE POINTS
■ 1. 'That you'
Normally a police officer will detect this offence and could therefore identify the offender to the court.
■ 2. 'not being at your place of abode. namely at ....'
■ 3. 'had with you'
Can be proved by showing that the accused had the article in his pocket or in a bag he was carrying or probably even in the car he was driving etc.
■ 4. 'a certain article namely a ....'.
Firstly, this point is proved by describing the article in question.

Secondly, if the article was made or adapted for use in committing a burglary, theft or cheat, then proof that he merely had such an article with him will be evidence that he had it with him for such a use.

Where the article is neither made or adapted for such a use then further evidence is needed to show why he had the article with him, eg a pedestrian stopped by a constable in a car park is found to have a large bunch of car keys with him.

The questioning may include the following: 'Where have you just come from?' 'Where are you going now?' 'What is your business in this car park?' 'Why do you need this large bunch of car keys?' 'Where did you get them all from?' etc. Depending on the answers follow-up inquiries may be necessary for verification purposes. Circumstantial evidence may be helpful and anyone who witnessed him trying a car door etc, could help to prove that the article, namely the bunch of keys, was for use in the course of burglary etc.

19. MAKING OFF WITHOUT PAYMENT
Section 3 Theft Act 1978

(A) POINTS TO PROVE
1. That you 2. knowing that payment on the spot was required or expected 3. for .... (enter the goods supplied or service done) 4. dishonestly 5. made off without having paid 6. with intent to avoid payment of .... (show amount) being the amount due.

(B) MEANING OF TERMS
■ 1. 'That you'
This means the person who enters the contract and 'bilks' or makes off.

■ 2. 'knowing that payment on the spot was required or expected'

'Knowing' means that the suspect was aware of the method of payment, eg at the end of a meal or after filling the petrol tank. This is the same whether someone asks for the payment (required) or the practice is for the customer to go to a cash desk to pay (expected). 'Payment on the spot' includes payment at the time of collecting goods on which work had been done (a clock repair) or a service had been provided (dry cleaning).

■ 3. 'for .... (enter the goods supplied or service done)'

The more common goods and services involved in this offence include drinks, meals (sitdown and take away), petrol, taxi rides, public transport, haircuts etc.

■ 4. 'dishonestly'

It should be noted that the definition of 'dishonesty' under section 2 Theft Act 1968 does not apply to this offence. A general definition of 'dishonesty' was provided in *R v Ghosh* [1982] 2 All ER 689, ie the court must decide whether:

(a) what was done was dishonest according to the ordinary standards of reasonable and honest people, and

(b) if so, did the defendant himself, realise that his actions were, according to those standards, dishonest.

■ 5. 'makes off without having paid'

This means a departure from the 'spot' where payment is required, therefore it would be difficult to commit this offence if goods or services were delivered or provided at one's home address. The essence of the offence is someone sneaking, running or driving away.

■ 6. 'with intent to avoid payment of .... (show amount) being the amount due'.

Means that the prosecution must show a guilty mind or *mens rea*. The intent must be to permanently avoid payment.

This offence is not committed where the intent is only to defer or delay payment.

(C) USUAL METHODS OR PROVING THESE POINTS

■ 1. 'That you'

Proving the person's identity can be a problem because unless witnesses can give a good description or other identifying information, the suspect, when caught, could always deny being the person who 'bilked'. Video camera pictures may be helpful, when available, together with car registration numbers. Therefore the suspect's identity would be proved in the witness statement(s) or the police officer's statement/interview record.

■ 2. 'knowing that payment on the spot was required or expected'

The customary practice regarding payment may need explaining in a witness statement. This could be strengthened by an admission from the suspect during interview that he was aware of the system of payment.

■ 3. 'for .... (enter the goods supplied or service done)'

Again a witness statement as follows would suffice.

'I saw the driver of the Ford Focus saloon, registered number, ABC 123 park at the non-leaded pump number 6 and fill the petrol tank of the car. My register showed he had put 40 litres of petrol into the car's petrol tank ....'

■ 4. 'dishonestly'

The prosecution case would be strongest if both elements of 'dishonesty' could be proved, ie that what was done was dishonest according to the ordinary standards of reasonable and honest people, eg leaving a petrol station without paying would obviously be contrary to the behaviour of honest people; AND that the accused himself realised that his actions were dishonest by those standards, eg proved by question and answer during the interview: 'Have you used self-service petrol stations before?' 'Did you realise it was dishonest to drive off without paying?'

■ 5. 'make off without having paid'

The witness statement(s) would prove this point supplemented by any video recording of the event or the accused's admission.

■ **6. 'with intent to avoid payment of .... (show amount) being the amount due'.**

Proving the state of a person's mind is more difficult than proving the state of his stomach. Failing an outright admission that he intended to permanently avoid payment, then circumstantial evidence may have to be relied upon. The phrase *'res ipsa loquitur'* (the thing speaks for itself) springs to mind as 'running out' of a restaurant or 'driving off' from a petrol station, without paying, should speak for itself, as far as 'intent' is concerned. However, the prosecution should remember the onus is on them to prove the required intent.

(D) SUPPORTING EVIDENCE

This offence is not committed where the supplying of the goods or the doing of the service is contrary to law, or payment for the service is not legally enforceable, eg where a taxi driver refuses to complete a journey, thereby breaching the contract. Where a person is 'making off' and is stopped before he succeeds, then an attempted 'making off' could be considered.

This offence is not an arrestable offence under the Police and Criminal Evidence Act but a power of arrest under section 3(4) of the Theft Act 1978 provides: 'Any person may arrest without warrant anyone who is or whom he reasonably suspects to be committing or attempting to commit this offence.'

20. ROBBERY

Section 8 Theft Act 1968

(A) POINTS TO PROVE

1. That you 2. did steal 3. and immediately before or at the time of doing so 4. and in order to do so 5. used force or put or sought to put a person in fear of being then and there subjected to force.

(B) MEANING OF TERMS

■ 1. 'That you'

Means the person who is suspected of the robbery.

■ 2. 'did steal'

Means the same as the offence of theft, see offence 13.

■ 3. 'and immediately before or at the time of doing so'

This refers to the use of **force** or seeking to put a person in **fear**, which we will call the 'FF' factor. Where the FF factor does not exist immediately before or at the time of the theft, then robbery is not committed. Lesser offences such as theft and assault would have to be considered.

■ 4. 'and in order to do so'

This means that the use or threat of force must relate to the theft. Where the accused and victim had had a fight and as an afterthought the accused stole the victim's wallet, this would not be robbery. Likewise, where a victim pursues a thief and is assaulted in order to stop his pursuit, this will not amount to robbery.

■ 5. 'used force or put or sought to put a person in fear of being them and there subjected to force'.

This point means that a person has had force used on him or the accused has put or sought to put a person in fear of immediate force. Examples of force include snatching an earring and tearing the ear in the process; snatching a handbag and spraining the victim's wrist in the process or punching a wife in order to steal the husband's brief case. Example of fear include the accused threatening to hit the victim unless he hands over his watch; or offering to punch a karate expert unless he hands over his wallet.

This last example has been used to illustrate that as long as the accused sought to put a person in fear, it is not necessary to prove that he was actually put in fear.

Note that force or threat of force against the pet dog, or a car would not amount to robbery. A 'person' must be subjected to force or put or sought to be put in fear of force.

(C) USUAL METHODS OF PROVING THESE POINTS

■ 1. 'That you'

This will be proved from witness statements or via the interview.

■ 2. 'did steal'

This should be proved as in the offence of theft, see offence 13.

■ 3. 'and immediately before or at the time of doing so'

The 'FF' factor ('force and 'fear', see (B)3 of this offence) must be proved to exist at the time of the theft or immediately before, eg, 'The man punched me in the stomach before he took my shopping bag' or, 'He frightened me with a knife as he took my motor bike.'

■ 4. 'and in order to do so'

Normally the FF factor will obviously relate to the theft but where any possible doubt exists, this point needs careful handling in the victim's statement and the accused's interview.

■ 5.'uses force or puts or seeks to put a person in fear of being them and there subjected to force'.

The victim's statement, together with that of any witness, should prove any force used, eg 'The man pushed me heavily to the ground before snatching my handbag'. The problem is one where a person was not put in fear and the prosecution must prove that the accused sought to put a person in fear etc. Again witness statements will prove this point eg, 'I heard the man shout at the young man "You'll never play tennis again after I've broken your legs, if you don't give me your bloody bag"', or better still an admission from the accused.

(D) SUPPORTING EVIDENCE

Note. Other offences to consider in circumstances not amounting to robbery are blackmail, offensive weapons, firearms, assault and theft. Also assault with intent to rob and attempted robbery may be committed.

21. UNLAWFUL POSSESSION OF A CONTROLLED DRUG
Section 5 Misuse of Drugs Act 1971

(A) POINTS TO PROVE
1. That you 2. did have in your possession 3. a controlled drug, namely .... (show name of drug)

(B) MEANING OF TERMS
■ 1. 'That you'
Means the person suspected of possessing a controlled drug.

■ 2. 'did have in your possession'
The word 'possession' has been given a wider meaning than would be commonly perceived. Under section 37 of the Misuse of Drugs Act 1971, which is the interpretation section of the Act, subsection (3) provides that 'possession' shall include anything subject to the control of the accused which is in the custody of another. Eg the accused leaving drugs at his mother or girlfriend's house provided the accused maintains 'control' over the drugs.

The mental element of this offence is dealt with in section 28 which provides that lack of **knowledge** can be a defence. Therefore the prosecution must prove that the accused had knowledge of the 'possession' and that the substance was a 'controlled drug'.

Once proved the defendant must convince the court that he - neither knew of,
 - nor suspected,
 - nor had reason to suspect,
the existence of some fact alleged by the prosecution. Eg, where the prosecution proves that he had cannabis resin in his hold-all and the accused proves someone put it there without his knowledge OR where it is proved that the substance was a class B amphetamine and the defendant convinces the court that he believed the tablets to be normal painkillers.

Two more defences exist which are pertinent to this offence, ie knowing or suspecting it to be a controlled drug,

(i) where the accused takes possession to prevent another from committing an offence. The proviso is that he should take all reasonable steps to destroy it or deliver it to a person lawfully entitled to take custody of it, as soon as possible after taking possession of it, or

(ii) taking possession for the purpose of delivering it to a person lawfully entitled to take custody of it, as soon as possible after taking possession of it.

A further defence which needs to be borne in mind is that of being authorised by regulations to possess it.

■ **3. 'a controlled drug, namely .... (show name of drug)'.**
This means any substance which is specified in Part I, II or III of Schedule 2 of the Misuse of Drugs Act 1971.

Part I deals with class A drugs - Class A includes: cocaine, diamorphine, lysergide (LSD), morphine, opium, whether raw, prepared or medicinal, pethidine.

Part II deals with Class B drug - Class B includes: amphetamine, cannabis and cannabis resin, dihydrocodine, ethymorphine (3-ethy/morphine).

Part III deals with Class C drugs - Class C includes: alprazolam, bromazepam, cathine, diazepam.

(C) USUAL METHODS OF PROVING THESE POINTS
■ **1. 'That you'**
This point is normally proved by the arresting officer identifying the suspect from a search or by questions and answers and later verification.

■ **2. 'did have in your possession'**
Most offences of possessing drugs come to light as a result of a search under section 23 of the Act. Therefore a statement from the searching officer or a police surgeon after an 'intimate search' would prove this point.

An 'intimate search' is searching the body orifices, other than the mouth. Where the substance is found elsewhere than on his person a statement from the person who found it together with evidence to show it was under the 'control' of the accused would be necessary. 'Control' could be proved in other witness statements or during interview with the accused. Eg, a statement from the accused's aunt, 'He always told me to keep the box hidden and not to open it.'

A person who gave directions to a supplier after which he received a parcel of drugs through his letter-box, 'possesses' the drug at the time it is put through the letter-box, *R v Peaston* [1979] Crim LR 183.

It was held in *R v Strong and Berry* [1989] *The Times* 26 January, that being present in the same car as cannabis is not proof of possession per se. This is so even if someone had said there was cannabis in the car.

■ **3. 'a controlled drug, namely .... (show name of drug)'.**
Proof of this point is generally the task of the scenes of crime officer and forensic science laboratories. Continuity is important and each stage of the suspected substance's journey from the suspect's pocket to a forensic science laboratory and back to the investigating officer should be carefully proved in witness statements. However in *R v Chatwood* [1980] 1 All ER 467, it was held that it was *prima facie* evidence of a substance being a controlled drug for an experienced drug user to admit possession of a substance which he identified as a controlled drug.

(D) SUPPORTING EVIDENCE

Note. There are many exemptions to possessing a controlled drug under the Misuse of Drugs Regulations 1985. Examples include constables, carriers, Post Office employees, Customs and Excise officers, laboratory staff etc, when acting in the course of their duties.

22. POSSESSION OF A CONTROLLED DRUG WITH INTENT TO SUPPLY
Section 5(3) Misuse of Drugs Act 1971

(A) POINTS TO PROVE
1. That you 2. did have in your possession 3. a controlled drug, namely .... [show name of drug] 4. whether lawfully or not 5. with intent to supply it to another.

(B) MEANING OF TERMS
■ **1, 2 and 3**
See meanings at offence 21, Possessing a controlled drug'.
■ **4. whether lawfully or not**
Means that someone in lawful possession, such as a pharmacist or doctor, could commit this offence.
■ **5. with intent to supply it to another.**
'Intent' is that 'state of mind' we have met in previous offences. The prosecution must show a guilty mind or *mens rea*. It has been held to be 'an intent to supply' where a person to whom a drug had been deposited for safe keeping intended to return to the person who gave it to him (*R v Maginnis* [1987] AC 303).

(C) USUAL METHOD OF PROVING THESE POINTS
■ **1, 2 and 3**
See methods at offence 21, Possessing a controlled drug.
■ **4. whether lawfully or not**
Whether the defendant had lawful or unlawful possession can be proved by questions and answers in the interview with the defendant. Other witness statements could prove this point if necessary. For example where a defendant remained silent an expert witness may prove lawful possession.
■ **5. with intent to supply it to another.**
An outright admission by the accused is usually the best evidence,

followed by circumstantial evidence from witnesses as to the intent, lifestyle and property owned etc.

There is a wealth of case law on this point, for example:

(a) Frequent visits to the defendant's house and persons carrying packets. A subsequent search of the house revealed large amounts of cash and some drugs and the occupant had not had paid employment for some years. The court held that it was contrary to common sense for the jury to be directed to ignore all these matters. The jury should by invited to look at the overall picture and draw such inferences as seem proper.

(b) The courts have stated that such issues must be reviewed on a case-by-case basis.

(c) It has been held that evidence of large amounts of money in the possession of the accused and an extravagant lifestyle - which on the face of it are derived from drug dealing - is admissible to help establish or otherwise the 'intent to supply' (*R v Morris* [1994] 159 JP1).

23. ABSTRACTING ELECTRICITY
Section 13 Theft Act 1968

(A) POINTS TO PROVE
1. That you 2. dishonestly 3. used without due authority (or dishonestly caused to be wasted or diverted) 4. any electricity.

(B) MEANING OF TERMS
1. 'That you'
Means the identity of the person abstracting electricity.
■ 2. 'dishonestly'
Basically, dishonestly means abstracted without a claim of right made in good faith. See offence 13(B)2, Theft, for a fuller definition.

■ 3. 'used without due authority (or dishonestly caused to be wasted or diverted)'

'Used without due authority' means to operate electrical appliances etc after passing by the meter or using the same coin or card continuously where the meter has been damaged or tampered with or by using the 'black box', etc. The black box entails inserting probes as the supply enters the meter, thereby stopping the meter registering the correct amount of electricity used.

'Dishonestly caused to be wasted or diverted' means, for example, unlawfully switching on electric storage heaters and lights at a place of employment to settle an old score with the owner, or running electricity to earth to flatten a battery etc.

■ 4. 'any electricity'.

This point is not defined but in the absence of judicial help it is considered that all types of electricity would be covered by this offence, ie alternating current from the national grid; privately produced electricity from a domestic generator; large standby batteries for use in case of emergencies or small car or flash light batteries. The quantity used is of no relevance to the offence only to the punishment.

(C) USUAL METHOD OF PROVING THESE POINTS

■ 1. 'That you'

On many occasions it is an electricity company employee who reports such offences. Therefore identity would be covered in his statement and backed up from the police interview.

■ 2.'dishonestly'

This point is proved by asking the suspect if he had any right or authority to abstract the electricity. In *R v McCreadie and Tume* [1992] Crim LR 872 a disconnected meter was unlawfully reconnected. It was held that for 'dishonestly' it was sufficient to prove that the electricity was used without the authority of the electricity company, with no intention to pay.

More in-depth questioning may be required for a 'wasting' or 'diverting' of electricity. In such cases the motive may help to prove a deliberate 'wasting' or 'diverting'.

■ **3. 'used without due authority (or dishonestly caused to be wasted or diverted)'**

Can be proved by an explanation in the electricity company's employee's statement, as to how the electricity was abstracted. For example: 'On opening the meter cupboard I saw that a "black box" was attached to the live wires just before entering the meter which I removed and pointed out to PC Peter Frost...'.

'Dishonestly wasting' could be proved by a witness who could say, 'I am the school caretaker and the boy I know to be Matthew Lowery, who had been in the detention room, deliberately followed me around the school turning the electric heaters back on as I turned them off for the night...'.

■ **4. 'any electricity'.**

Proof that electricity was present is necessary before the prosecution could prove an abstraction. Therefore the electricity company witness could say how much or estimate how much electricity had been abstracted. This point may be more difficult to prove where generators or batteries are involved.

As the quantity used is not an element of the offence, the mere proof of a light being illuminated for whatever period, would appear to be sufficient for an abstraction.

24. PASSING COUNTERFEIT NOTES AND COINS
Section 15 Forgery and Counterfeiting Act 1981

(A) POINTS TO PROVE
1. That you 2. did pass (or tender) as genuine 3. anything which is and which you knew or believed to be 4. a counterfeit of a currency note (or of a protected coin).

(B) MEANING OF TERMS

■ 1. 'That you'

Means the person passing the counterfeit money.

■ 2. 'did pass (or tender) as genuine'

Means the putting into circulation of the counterfeit money (even if it was immediately rejected as being a counterfeit).

Note that passing or tendering is not restricted to passing or tendering it as legal tender.

■ 3. 'anything which is and which he knew or believed to be'

For this offence to be committed the counterfeit money – must in fact be counterfeit, and - the accused must know it is counterfeit, or - he must believe it to be counterfeit.

■ 4. 'a counterfeit of a currency note (or of a protected coin)'.

'Counterfeit' means something that is not a currency note or a protected coin but resembles one of them (whether on one side only or on both) to such an extent that it is reasonably capable of passing for a currency note or protected coin, or if it is a currency note or protected coin which has been so altered that it is reasonably capable of passing for a currency note or protected coin of some other description.

'Currency note' means any note which has been lawfully issued in this country or the Republic of Ireland AND is or had been used as money in the country where it was issued AND is payable on demand OR any note which has been lawfully issued in a country other than those above AND is used as money in that country.

'Protected Coin' is any coin which is used as money in any country or is specified in an order made by the Treasury for the purpose of Part II of this Act (Forgery and Counterfeiting Act 1981).

(C) USUAL METHOD OF PROVING THESE POINTS

■ 1. 'That you'

This may be proved by the shopkeeper, bank cashier, bar person to whom the counterfeit money passed or was offered.

■ 2. 'did pass (or tender) as genuine'

This point can be proved by the circumstances of the passing as recorded in the witness statement(s).

■ 3. 'anything which is and which he knows or believes to be'

Guilty knowledge can be proved from his admissions or from a continued act of passing such money after being told the money is counterfeit

For example, the accused was told by the petrol station staff that a £20 note was counterfeit as identified by a machine. Nevertheless he tried to pay a bill at the newsagent's with a similar £20 note where he again was told that the note was imperfect at the watermark. Undaunted he paid the remaining £20 notes into his bank account and was again told by the bank that they were counterfeit. This evidence of passing after he knew or at least believed the notes were counterfeit would help to prove his state of mind.

■ 4. 'a counterfeit of a currency note (or of a protected coin)'.

Normally the note should be seized and forwarded to New Scotland Yard for expert examination. If counterfeit, the necessary statements to prove continuity from being passed, to being returned to the officer in the case will be needed. Forensic Science departments can also advise regarding suspect money and force instructions/guidance should be consulted.

(D) SUPPORTING EVIDENCE

Note 1. The offence under section 16 of the Act covers the circumstance of being given counterfeit money in change, for example, and then knowingly trying to pass it on or tender it as genuine.

Note 2. Where a person intends to hand in such money, there may be a defence - but not when the person cannot make up his or her mind as to the course of action to take (*R v Sunman* [1995] Crim LR 569).

Section 3

Miscellaneous offences

1. DOGS WORRYING LIVESTOCK
Section 1 Dogs (Protection of Livestock) Act 1953

(A) POINTS TO PROVE
1. That you 2. being the owner (or person in charge)
3. of a dog which worried 4. livestock .... (specify)
5. on certain agricultural land at .... (specify).

(B) MEANING OF TERMS
■ 1. 'That you'
Means the identity of the offender.
■ 2. 'being the owner (or person in charge)'
Note that only the owner can commit this offence unless the
dog is in the charge of another person, in which case the other
would also commit the offence. Where the offence takes place
when the dog is in another's charge the owner will not be liable
if he proves that it was in the charge of some other person
whom he reasonably believed to be a fit and proper person to be
in charge of the dog.
■ 3. 'of a dog which worried'
'Worried' means (a) attacking livestock; or (b) chasing livestock
in such a way as may reasonably be expected to cause injury or
suffering to the livestock or, in the case of females, abortion, or
loss of or diminution in their produce.
■ 4. 'livestock .... (specify)'
'Livestock' means cattle, sheep, goats, swine, horses or poultry;
'cattle' means bulls, cows, oxen, heifers or calves; 'horses'
includes asses and mules; 'poultry' means domestic fowls,
turkeys, geese or ducks.
■ 5. 'on certain agricultural land at .... (specify)'.
'Agricultural land' means land used as arable, meadow or graz-
ing land or for the purposes of poultry farming, pig farming,
market gardens, allotments, nursery grounds or orchards.

(C) USUAL METHODS OF PROVING THESE POINTS

■ 1. 'That you'

Is proved by identifying the owner or person in charge of the dog. This point sometimes causes problems because of the owner's absence when the dog is worrying hens or sheep etc. In these cases it may be necessary to trace the dog to a particular house and then arrange for any witness(es) to see the dog at the house in order to identify the dog and, thereby, the owner.

■ 2. 'being the owner (or person in charge)'

This point is proved by questions to the defendant such as, 'Are you the owner of this dog?' 'Who buys the dog's food?' or 'Where does the dog sleep or live?' Where it is suspected that the owner had left the dog with another person when the worrying took place, a statement from the owner saying who he had left in charge of the dog would be necessary.

■ 3. 'of a dog which worried'

'Worried' is proved by a witness stating he saw the dog in question attacking livestock or chasing in such a way as may reasonably be expected adversely to affect the livestock as outlined at (B) 3 ante. A statement may be required from an expert witness to prove the possible effects of chasing. If the owner of the livestock, such as a farmer, is not able to give such evidence, consideration could be given to calling a veterinary surgeon. If the dog is not caught in the act of worrying, circumstantial evidence regarding the dog's condition when finally seen could be important. For example in the case of a hen the dog could be examined for the presence of feathers, blood, hen droppings, mud or hen food etc on its muzzle, paws or body.

■ 4. 'livestock .... (specify)'

Evidence must be available that the animal(s) 'worried' was one mentioned in the definition of 'livestock' as defined at (B) 4 ante

■ 5. 'on certain agricultural land at .... (specify)'.

This point is proved by showing in a witness statement that the land where the 'worrying' took place was land mentioned in the definition of 'agricultural land' at (B)5 of this offence.

2. POSSESSING ETC SHOTGUN WITHOUT A CERTIFICATE

Section 2 Firearms Act 1968

(A) POINTS TO PROVE

1. That you 2. not being a person exempted from the requirements of the Firearms Act 1968 3. did have in your possession (or purchase or acquire) a shotgun 4. without holding a certificate under the said Act authorising you to possess shotguns.

(B) MEANING OF TERMS

■ 1. 'That you'

Means the identity of the person possessing the shotgun.

■ 2. 'not being a person exempted from the requirements of the Firearms Act 1968'

Briefly, exempted persons include:

(a) those in possession of a police permit;

(b) firearms dealers or their employees;

(c) auctioneers, carriers or warehousemen etc;

(d) licensed slaughtermen etc;

(e) those possessing for sporting, athletic and other approved activities, eg at rifle club or range;

(f) those borrowing shotguns from an occupier to use on the private premises of the occupier in his presence;

(g) those shooting at artificial targets with a shotgun with police approval;

(h) those using firearms in connection with the theatre and/or cinema;

(i) those using firearms connected with equipment for ships and aircraft;

(j) those with a visitor's firearm permit issued under section 17 of the 1988 Act;

(k) those holding Northern Irish certificates for shotguns.

Note that an antique firearm will not be a shotgun for the purposes of this offence. Whether the shotgun is antique will be a question of fact and degree in each case. However, if it is honestly and reasonably believed to be an antique it matters not if it is not in fact an antique.

■ 3. 'did have in your possession (or purchase, or acquire) a shotgun'

'Possession' used in this offence means having control and would probably cover the much wider circumstances of possession than the phrase 'has with him' would allow. Possession at home or elsewhere would most likely suffice.

'Shotgun' is defined as a smooth-bore gun within the meaning of this Act, that is to say, a smooth-bore gun which has a barrel not less than 24 inches in length and does not have a barrel with a bore exceeding two inches in diameter and either has no magazine or has a non-detachable magazine incapable of holding more than two cartridges and is not a revolver gun. This definition under the Firearms (Amendment) Act 1988 effectively makes into section one firearms, cannons, pump-action and semi-automatic shotguns with a magazine capacity of more than two cartridges and bolt-action shotguns having any capacity of more than two cartridges.

■ 4. 'without holding a certificate under the said Act authorising you to possess shotguns'.

'Shotgun certificate' under this Act means a certificate granted by a chief officer of police under this Act and authorising a person to possess shotguns.

(C) USUAL METHODS OF PROVING THESE POINTS
■ 1. 'That you'

Is proved by identifying the defendant in a witness statement. These offences generally come to light when outstanding renewals of shotgun certificates are enquired into, therefore the witness concerned will usually be the officer dealing with the case.

■ 2. 'not being a person exempted from the requirements of the Firearms Act 1968'

This point would be put forward by the defendant and it would be for the prosecution to disprove the alleged exemption. For example, if a false allegation was made to the effect that he had borrowed the shotgun under the exemption as at point (B)2(f) of this offence, the prosecution would try to disprove the claim by taking a statement from the occupier of the land.

■ 3. 'did have in your possession (or purchase or acquire) a shotgun'

This point is usually proved by a witness stating the defendant was carrying the shotgun or it was found at his home or in his car. Proving that the firearm in question is a shotgun should not cause problems, but if in doubt expert evidence could be sought.

■ 4. 'without holding a certificate under the said Act authorising you to possess shotguns'.

This point is similar in type to the proving of a 'no insurance' offence under the Road Traffic Act. In other words the defendant could have obtained a shotgun certificate from any one of several chief officers of police, or insurance from one of many companies. In order to save the prosecution proving the almost impossible fact that the defendant was not the holder of a certificate a negative averment can be made. This means that the onus is on the defendant to prove he has such a certificate as that particular knowledge is peculiar to him.

The prosecution evidence will, therefore, usually consist of a witness stating that the defendant was unable to produce a certificate and/or admitted he did not have such a certificate.

3. DISCHARGING FIREARM NEAR HIGHWAY

Section 161(2) Highways Act 1980

(A) POINTS TO PROVE

1. That you 2. did, without lawful authority or excuse
3. discharge a firearm 4. within 50 feet of the centre of
.... 5. a highway which comprises (or consists of) a
carriageway 6. in consequence whereof users of the
highway (or (specify person) a user of the highway) were
(or was) injured (or interrupted, or endangered).

(B) MEANING OF TERMS

■ **1. 'That you'**

Means the identity of the offender.

■ **2. 'did, without lawful authority or excuse'**

Means that the defendant had no authority under the law, eg a
policeman in the execution of his duty when killing an escaped
bullock on a highway. 'Excuse' could for example apply to the
owner of livestock killing a stray dog within 50 feet of the centre
of a highway to stop the dog worrying his sheep.

■ **3. 'discharge a firearm'**

In the absence of a case to the contrary, discharge apparently
means to fire the gun or firearm, and firearm apparently means
any lethal barrelled weapon of any description from which any
shot, bullet or other missile can be discharged.

■ **4. 'within 50 feet of the centre of .... '**

This distance is measured from the centre of the carriageway in
question and the discharging must take place within that distance.

■ **5. 'a highway which comprises (or consists of) a carriageway'**

'Carriageway' means a way contributing to or comprised in a
highway, being a way (other than a cycle track) over which the
public have a right of way for the passage of vehicles (Highways
Act 1980). Therefore footpaths etc on which the public cannot
take vehicles are not 'carriageways'.

■ **6. 'in consequence whereof users of the highway (or (specify person) a user of the highway) were (or was) injured (or interrupted, or endangered)'.**

This point means that as a result of the discharge of the firearm any user(s) of the highway were:

(a) actually injured; or

(b) interrupted, eg having to take a different route or take shelter etc; or

(c) endangered, eg any missile passing near to the user(s) so as to be dangerous.

(C) USUAL METHODS OF PROVING THESE POINTS

■ **1. 'That you'**

Is proved by a witness identifying the defendant.

■ **2. 'did, without lawful authority or excuse'**

This point is for the defence to raise and, if raised, for the prosecution to disprove.

■ **3. 'discharge a firearm'**

Can be proved by a witness stating in his statement of evidence the fact that he saw and heard etc the defendant fire the gun. The defendant might admit discharging the gun or circumstantial evidence (such as broken street lamps and panes of glass in bus shelter windows or dented cars etc) might be of assistance.

■ **4. 'within 50 feet of the centre of ....'**

This point is proved by measuring the 50 feet from the centre of the carriageway and showing, perhaps in the police officer's statement, how far the distance extended. The physical position of the defendant should then be proved to be within the required 50 feet. This could be done in the statement of perhaps another witness who actually saw where the defendant was standing or, failing this, the position could be proved from the defendant's own admission.

■ **5. 'a highway which comprises (consists of) a carriageway'**

This point is proved by showing the public had a right of way for the passage of vehicles (being other than a cycle track) in accordance with the definition at point (B)5 of this offence. For example '.......... within 50 feet of the centre of Regent's Street'.

■ **6. 'in consequence whereof users of the highway (or (specify person) a user of the highway) were (or was) injured (or interrupted, or endangered)'.**

Is proved by showing in a witness statement for example: 'I was hit by an air-gun pellet on my left forearm, which caused a slight cut, while walking in High Street' or, 'I had to duck to avoid being hit by air-gun pellets when I cycled in Queen's Street. I was in danger of being hit by a pellet'.

(D) SUPPORTING EVIDENCE

Note. The offences of trespassing with a firearm contrary to section 20 Firearms Act 1968 and carrying a firearm in a public place contrary to section 19 Firearms Act 1968 are both similar to the Highways Act offence. But the Highways Act offence fills the gap where the defendant is neither trespassing (section 20) or in a public place (section 19), eg when in his own front garden.

4. DRINKING UNDER AGE
Section 169 Licensing Act 1964

(A) POINTS TO PROVE
1. That you 2. being a person under 18, namely .... years 3. did in licensed premises 4. consume 5. intoxicating liquor, namely .... 6. in a bar.

(B) MEANING OF TERMS
■ **1. 'That you'**
Means the person consuming the intoxicating liquor.

■ **2. 'being a person under 18 namely .... years'**

Means that the eighteenth birthday has not yet been attained. A person attains a particular age at the commencement of the relevant anniversary of the date of his birth, per section 9 Family Law Reform Act 1969.

■ **3. 'did in licensed premises'**

This point means, unless the context otherwise requires, a reference to premises for which a justices' licence (or occasional licence) is in force and as including a reference to any premises in respect of which a notice under section 199(c) of this Act is for the time being in force (ie theatres) per section 200 Licensing Act 1964.

■ **4. 'consume'**

This point means drink the intoxicating liquor.

■ **5. 'intoxicating liquor, namely .... '**

Means spirits, wine, beer, cider and any fermented, distilled or spirituous liquor but (apart from cider) does not include any liquor for the sale of which by wholesale no excise licence is required. (Cider includes perry.) Where beer and lemonade is mixed into a 'shandy' at the time of sale it is 'intoxicating liquor'. In *Hall v Hyder* [1966] 1 All ER 661 it was held that where the barman mixes the beer and lemonade at the time of the sale it will be 'intoxicating liquor' notwithstanding that the overall alcoholic content is less than two degrees proof. If a bottled shandy is purchased and it is under two degrees proof, the drink will not be 'intoxicating liquor'.

■ **6. 'in a bar'.**

Includes any place exclusively or mainly used for the sale and consumption of intoxicating liquor (section 201(1) Licensing Act 1964).

(C) USUAL METHODS OF PROVING THESE POINTS
■ **1. 'That you'**

Identification by the police officer.

■ 2. 'being a person under 18 namely............ years'

The vast majority of under-age drinking offences are detected during routine visits to public houses by a sergeant and one or two constables. Persons who are consuming in the bar and who look under 18 may be asked 'What is your date of birth?' Their answer can be recorded in the officer's pocket book together with the result of a check of the suspected offender's birth certificate. In cases of difficulty a statement from someone present at the birth is good evidence.

■ 3. 'did in licensed premises'

In practice this point is proved by referring to the premises concerned as licensed premises, eg, 'At 14.40 hours on Friday 26 September 1980 I entered the bar lounge of the licensed premises, the Bull's Head in Main Road, Notown', and should there be any doubt the licence should be examined. Failure to produce the justices' licence, occasional licence or general or special order of exemption is an offence (section 185 Licensing Act 1964).

■ 4. 'consume'

This point is proved by asking the suspect, 'Is this your drink?' and recording the fact that some drink had been taken from the glass. Note that section 196 Licensing Act 1964 provides that evidence that consumption of intoxicating liquor was about to take place shall be evidence of the consumption without proof of actual consumption.

■ 5. 'intoxicating liquor, namely............'

The type of liquor should be noted. The defendant can be asked, 'What are you drinking?' In cases of difficulty the licensee or person who served the drink can be questioned or the drink analysed by experts.

■ 6. 'in a bar'.

Is usually proved by, 'I saw the defendant in the bar of the Red Lion............'

5. FOUND DRUNK
Section 12 Licensing Act 1872

(A) POINTS TO PROVE
1. That you 2. were found 3. drunk 4. in a highway (or other public place or certain premises licensed for the sale of intoxicating liquors by retail) called............

(B) MEANING OF TERMS
■ 1. 'That you'
Means the identity of the accused.
■ 2. 'were found'
Means that for the offence to be committed the officer etc must 'find' the accused in a drunken state. The offence was designed to provide protection for the drunken person etc, so that, when sober, the accused could not be reported for his drunkenness.
■ 3. 'drunk'
This point means under the influence of alcohol to such an extent that a police officer would feel that the defendant was a liability to himself or other persons or property. There is no power of arrest for simple drunkenness but if the defendant is so drunk as to be incapable of taking care of himself then a power of arrest exists per section 1 Licensing Act 1902. This offence and power is therefore mainly used when a person is drunk and incapable.
■ 4. 'in a highway (or other public place or certain premises licensed for the sale of intoxicating liquors by retail) called............'.
'Highway' and 'licensed premises' are widely understood and, normally, cause no problems. Note that an occasional licence is included in the term 'licensed premises'. 'Other public place' means places other than highways to which the public have access whether on payment or otherwise. Persons found drunk inside a tramcar or hackney carriage would probably come within this offence.

(C) USUAL METHODS OF PROVING THESE POINTS

■ 1. 'That you'

Is proved by the officer dealing with the case identifying the defendant in his statement of evidence.

■ 2. 'were found'

This point is proved by the officer dealing with the case including in his statement words such as, 'I found the defendant on the pavement in the High Street'.

■ 3. 'drunk'

This point could be proved in the officer's statement by words, such as, 'Unsteady on his feet; could not walk; glassy eyed; breath smelling of alcohol; speech slurred; vomited on his clothing; urinated in his trousers' etc. All help to describe drunkenness or being drunk and incapable.

■ 4. 'in a highway (or other public place or certain premises licensed for the sale of intoxicating liquors by retail) called.............'.

This point is proved by describing in the officer's statement the place where the defendant was found, ie (a) a 'highway' such as King Street, or Oxford Street; or (b) 'other public place' such as a football ground or railway station; or (c) 'licensed premises' such as the Three Legs public house or the Swan and Talbot Inn.

6. DRUNK AND DISORDERLY

Section 91(1) Criminal Justice Act 1967

(A) POINTS TO PROVE

1. That you 2. while drunk 3. in any public place namely .... 4. were guilty of disorderly behaviour.

(B) MEANING OF TERMS

■ 1. 'That you'

Means the identity of the defendant.

■ 2. 'while drunk'

Means that the defendant was under the influence of alcohol to such an extent that a police officer would feel that he could be described as drunk.

■ 3. 'in any public place, namely ....'

'Public place' is defined as including any highway and any other premises or place to which at the material time the public have or are permitted to have access, whether on payment or otherwise (section 91(4) Criminal Justice Act 1967). Such places as the public rooms of licensed premises during permitted hours and railway stations will be public places.

■ 4. 'were guilty of disorderly behaviour'.

There is no definition of this term but it is submitted that any conduct which is not orderly, such as a breach of the peace, would suffice. For example, shouting, waving arms about and interfering with other people's comfort would probably amount to disorderly behaviour.

(C) USUAL METHODS OF PROVING THESE POINTS

■ 1. 'That you'

Is usually proved by the police officer who is dealing with the case identifying the defendant.

■ 2. 'while drunk'

This point is usually proved in the police officer's statement by sentences such as, 'unsteady on his feet, glassy eyes, breath smelling of alcohol, speech slurred, untidy clothing, vomit on clothing, urinated in trousers etc'.

■ 3. 'in any public place namely............'

This point could be established by describing in the police officer's statement the place where the defendant was disorderly, eg, 'In High Street, at the first division football ground of.............', 'in the bar of the Red Lion during permitted hours etc'. In cases involving public places where the public are only admitted on payment etc the prosecution must prove that the place comes within the definition of public place at (B)3 of this offence.

■ 4. 'were guilty of disorderly behaviour'.

This point is established by observations in the police officer's statement to the effect. 'I told him to be quiet and go home but he refused, started shouting "Nazis, Nazis", and waved his arms about', or, 'I saw him trying to jump over the railings near the market place traffic lights and a crowd of people began to gather. I told him to stop and go home but he continued trying to jump the railings etc', or, 'I saw him pushing his way into a taxi queue and shouting "I am having the first taxi", I told him to go home quietly but he refused to stop pushing in front of people in the queue… etc'.

7. LITTER OFFENCE

Section 87 Environmental Protection Act 1990

(A) POINTS TO PROVE

1. That you **2.** did throw down (or drop or otherwise deposit) **3.** in (or into or from) .... (name place) a public open place **4.** and left there (name article) **5.** in such circumstances as to cause (or contribute to or tend to lead to) the defacement of a public open place .... (name place) by litter.

(B) MEANING OF TERMS

■ 1. 'That you'

Means the identity of the offender.

■ 2. 'did throw down (or drop or otherwise deposit)'

Means any method of 'depositing' litter.

In *Felix v DPP* [1998] Crim LR 657 it was held that 'otherwise deposits' had a wide meaning and 'deposits' means no more than 'places' or 'puts'.

■ 3. 'in (or into or from) ..... (name place) a public open place'

This point means to throw down etc in a public place IN the open air; or INTO a public place in the open air; or FROM a public place in the open air into another public place in the open air.

All the above must be to deface ANY PUBLIC OPEN PLACE. Examples include:

In -   throw down litter in park, highway or footpath.

Into -   litter thrown or deposited from a car or house window into a highway or footpath etc.

From - litter thrown from a park over the fence into the street.

This section applies to any public open place and, in so far as the place is not a public open place, also to the following places:

(a) any relevant highway or relevant road and any trunk road which is a special road;

(b) any place on relevant land of a principal litter authority;

(c) any place on relevant Crown land;

(d) any place on relevant land of any designated statutory undertaker;

(e) any place on relevant land of any designated educational institution;

(f)   any place on relevant land within a litter control area of a local authority.

In this section 'public open place' means a place in the open air to which the public are entitled or permitted to have access without payment; and any covered place open to the air on at least one side and available for public use shall be treated as a public open place. An example would be a bus shelter consisting of a roof and three sides. In *Felix v DPP* [1998] Crim LR 657 it was held that a telephone kiosk which had a door which was normally shut, was not 'a place in the open air.'

■ 4. 'and left there (name article)'

This point means 'left' and not necessarily 'abandoned' (*Witney v Cattanach* [1979] Crim LR 461). In this case the defendant was living in a tent near his lorry with his wife and seven children. He sorted through a pile of metal beside his parked lorry. It was held that the metal had been deposited and permitted to remain beside the road for such a time and in such circumstances that it could be said to have been left there. An article deposited with no intention to remove it could be found to have been left after it had been there only a short time.

■ **5. 'in such circumstances as to cause (or contribute to or tend to lead to) the defacement of a public open space (name place) by litter'.**

This point means that the litter must deface or contribute to or tend to lead to the defacement of a public open space. 'Public open space' is discussed at point (B)3 above.

(C) USUAL METHODS OF PROVING THESE POINTS

■ **1. 'That you'**

Is usually proved by a witness identifying the defendant etc.

■ **2. 'did throw down (or drop or otherwise deposit)'**

This point is usually proved by a witness stating that, 'I saw (the defendant) throw the fish and chip papers out of his car window on to the road', or, 'I saw (the defendant) throw a newspaper into my garden from the adjoining road'.

■ **3. 'in (or into or from) .... (name place) a public open space'**

Evidence of this point usually takes the form of a witness statement describing where the litter was thrown IN, INTO or FROM. It will be necessary to show the place was one in the open air to which the public had access without payment.

■ **4. 'and left there .... (name article)'**

The prosecution must be careful to show that the defendant had not just thrown down litter which he intended to collect later and dispose of lawfully. In the majority of cases the 'leaving' will be obvious, but help could be obtained from the decision in *Witney v Cattanach* at (B)4 of this offence in cases of difficulty.

■ 5. 'in such circumstances as to cause (or contribute to or tend to lead to) the defacement of a public open space (name place) by litter'.

This final point could be proved by a sentence in a witness statement to the effect that, 'The newspaper defaced (or contributed to or tended to lead to the defacement of) Kings Road (or my front garden)'. Note that the place defaced etc, need not be a public place, but merely one which is in the open air, eg some person's front garden (see (B)3 of this offence for meaning of 'public open space').

8. SPORTING EVENTS – CONTROL OF ALCOHOL

Section 2(1) Sporting Events (Control of Alcohol etc) Act 1985

(A) POINTS TO PROVE

1. That you 2. had intoxicating liquor (or an article to which this section applies) 3. in your possession 4. at a time during the period of a designated sporting event 5. while being in an area of a designated sports ground from which the event may be directly viewed, namely,..............

(B) MEANING OF TERMS

■ 1. 'That you'

Means the person who is in possession of intoxicating liquor.

■ 2. 'had intoxicating liquor (or an article to which this section applies)'

'Intoxicating liquor' has the same meaning as under section 201(1) Licensing Act 1964 (see offence 4(B)5, Drinking under age).

This section applies to any article capable of causing injury to a person struck by it, being :

(a) a bottle, can or other portable container (including such an article when crushed or broken) which -

    (i) is for holding any drink, and

    (ii) is of a kind, which, when empty, is normally discarded or returned to, or left to be recovered by, the supplier; or

(b) part of an article falling within paragraph (a) above: but does not apply to anything that is for holding any medical product (within the meaning of the Medicines Act).

■ 3. 'in your possession'

'Possession' appears to mean actually in the physical possession of the offender.

■ 4. 'at a time during the period of a designated sporting event'

A 'designated sporting event' means an event or proposed event which has been designated or is part of a class designated by order made by the Secretary of State. It also includes events designated under comparable Scottish legislation. Events which are to be held outside Great Britain can also be designated.

The 'period of a designated sporting event' means the period of time commencing two hours before the start of the event and ending one hour after the end of it. However if the start is delayed then the period commencing two hours before the advertised start is included. If an event is postponed or cancelled then the period in such a case is the period commencing two hours before the advertised start and ending one hour after that time.

Designation of sports grounds and events are dealt with as follows. The Sports Grounds and Sporting Events (Designation) Order 1985 designated the sports grounds and sporting events to which the Act applies.

The designated grounds are:

    (i) the home grounds of Football Association or Welsh Football Association football clubs;

(ii) any other ground in England and Wales used occasionally or temporarily by such a club;

(iii) any ground in England and Wales used for international football matches, as well as:

(iv) Wembley Stadium and Shielfield Park (Berwick-upon-Tweed).

The designated matches in England and Wales are:

(i) association football matches involving at least one Football League or Football Association Premier League club team and includes matches played by the reserve and youth teams of such a club;

(ii) international association football matches;

(iii) association football matches in the competition for the European Cup, the Cup Winners' Cup and the UEFA Cup;

(iv) matches within the jurisdiction of the Scottish Football Association. This covers the situation of Berwick Rangers who play in the Scottish League although their ground is in England.

Under section 9(6) of the Act sporting events in which all competitors take part without reward and to which all spectators are admitted free of charge are not subject to the provisions of the Act.

In England and Wales the provisions of the Act apply only if both the ground and the event are designated. The 1985 Order also designates the following two classes of football matches when they are held outside Great Britain:

(i) association football matches in which at least one team represents the Football Association, the Welsh Football Association or a Football League club team; and

(ii) football matches involving at least one Football Association or Welsh Football Association club team in the competition for the European Cup, the Cup Winners' Cup and UEFA Cup.

■ **5. 'while being in an area of a designated sports ground from which the event may be directly viewed, namely, ...'.**

A 'designated sports ground' means any place used for sporting events which has accommodation for spectators and which has been designated or is part of a class designated by the Secretary of State. The area of a ground from which an event may be directly viewed includes stands, terraces and any restaurants, sponsors' boxes and other rooms which overlook the pitch.

'Namely' would required a description of the place where the offender was seen, eg 'at the front of the stand in seat A24'.

(C) USUAL METHODS OF PROVING THESE POINTS

■ **1. 'That you'**

This point is normally proved by the police officer in his statement of evidence. For example: 'I saw a man I know to be Bob Robinson sitting in seat A24…'

■ **2. 'had intoxicating liquor (or an article to which this section applies)'**

The proof that a substance is intoxicating liquor will be similar to that required in offence 5 (Drinking under age). The question should be asked: 'What are you drinking?' In cases of difficulty the drink should be analysed by experts.

■ **3. 'in your possession'**

The police officer's evidence would prove this point, eg, 'I saw Mr Robinson holding a can of beer'.

■ **4. 'at a time during the period of a designated sporting event'.**

This can be proved by showing in the police officer's statement that the game being played was an association football match between two Football League clubs namely............

'During the period' can be proved by showing that the offence took place between the specified times, eg, 'The football game had begun 15 minutes before the offence'.

■ 5. 'while being in an area of a designated sports ground from which the event may be directly viewed, namely ....'.

'Designated sports ground' can be proved by including in the police officer's statement of evidence that the match was being played on the home ground of the Sometime United Football Club, a Football Association club.

'Directly viewed' can be proved by the police officer showing in his statement words to the effect that the pitch could be directly viewed from the stand where Mr Robinson was sitting.

(D) SUPPORTING EVIDENCE

Note 1. A power to search and arrest a suspect is provided under section 7(2) of the Act.

Note 2. Medical products as mentioned under (B)2 of this offence include substances which can be administered to animals for medical purposes.

9. TRESPASSING ON LAND
Section 61 Criminal Justice and Public Order Act 1994

(A) POINTS TO PROVE
1. That you 2. knowing 3. that a direction under subsection (1) of this section had been given
4. which applied to you 5. failed to leave the land
6. as soon as was reasonably practicable or
7. having left, again entered the land as a trespasser 8. within a period of three months
9. beginning with the day on which the direction was given.

(B) MEANING OR TERMS

■ **1. 'That you'** Means the identity of the offender.

■ **2. 'Knowing'**
Means that guilty knowledge is required and that the offender must be aware of the next point.

■ **3. 'that a direction under subsection (1) had been given'**
The 'direction' means that where a senior police officer present at the scene reasonably believes that:

(a) two or more persons are trespassing on land AND are present there with the common purpose of residing there for any period;

(a) that reasonable steps have been taken by or on behalf of the occupier, to ask them to leave;

AND

(a) that any of those persons has caused damage to the land or property thereon OR used threatening, abusive or insulting words or behaviour towards the occupier, a member of his family or an employee or agent of his, or

(b) that those persons have between them six or more vehicles on the land;

he (the senior police officer) may DIRECT those persons, or any of them, to leave the land and to remove any vehicles or other property they have with them on the land.

■ **4. 'Which applied to you'**
Means that the above direction applied to the offender.

■ **5. 'Failed to leave the land ....'**
Means in effect, not vacating the land described together with any vehicle or property he might have there.

■ **6. 'As soon as reasonably practicable'**
Means that if the trespasser has accumulated a lot of property on the land then common sense must prevail in allowing sufficient time for vacation.

■ **7. 'Having left, entered the land again as a trespasser'**
Means that the leaving was not final and that the trespasser had entered the same piece of land again, section 61(4).

■ **8.'Within a period of three months'**
Means three calendar months.

■ **9. 'beginning with the day on which the direction was given'.**
Means that the three calendar months starts with the day the trespasser was told to leave. Presumably no offence under section 61(4) will be committed if the trespasser returns after three months.

(C) USUAL METHODS OF PROVING THESE POINTS

■ **1. 'That you'**
Can be proved by asking the person his name and date of birth etc during the interview. Photographs or video could be considered or even the power of arrest where identity is a problem.

■ **2. 'knowing'**
Can be proved by asking the trespasser if he was aware that he had been directed to leave the land. If the trespasser is not co-operative then a statement from the officer giving or communicating news of the direction, or some other witness, could help prove this point.

■ **3. 'that a direction under subsection (1) etc has been given.'**
This point would be best proved by an admission from the trespasser that the direction had been given or from a statement from the officer giving the direction.

■ **4. 'which applied to you'**
Can be proved in a statement from the occupier of the land or the officer dealing with the case, to the effect that the direction was made, was communicated and was pertinent to the trespasser or during the interview with the trespasser.

■ **5. 'failed to leave the land**
Would be obvious to all concerned and a statement to that effect from a witness would suffice fully describing the land eg – 'The five-acre field adjacent to Plum Tree Farm'.

■ **6. 'as soon as reasonably practicable'**
This point can be proved by setting a reasonable period for the

trespasser to vacate the land and showing such a period in the police officer's statement - OR

■ **7. 'having left again enters the land as a trespasser'**
Can be proved by showing in the police officer's statement or some other witness' statement that the trespasser left the land but entered again without permission, ie as a trespasser.

■ **8. 'within a period of three months'**
Proved by showing the date on which the direction to leave was given and the date of re-entry in a witness' statement.

■ **9. 'beginning with the day on which the direction was given'.**
Proved as above.

(D) SUPPORTING EVIDENCE

Note 1. Section 61(2) of the Criminal Justice and Public Order Act 1994 also provides that where the senior police officer believes that the persons on the land were not originally trespassers - but have since become trespassers - the officer must reasonably believe that the subsection (1) conditions are satisfied after those persons become trespassers, before he can give a subsection (1) direction.

The subsection (1) conditions include damage or threats etc (see (B)3 of this offence) and note that damage includes the deposit of any substance capable of polluting the land.

Once the direction has been given, any police officer at the scene (not just the senior police officer) can communicate news of it to the trespassers.

Note 2. A power of arrest exists for a constable in uniform who reasonably suspects that a person is committing the above offence.

Note 3. A defence is provided viz: if the accused shows he was not trespassing on the land or that he had a reasonable excuse for failing to leave the land as soon as reasonably practicable or for re-entering the land as a trespasser. Such reasonable excuses could be the presence of the elderly, invalids, pregnant women, children etc and the police may wish to take such matters into account when dealing with this offence.

Note 4. Among other definitions, 'vehicle' is defined as any vehicle, whether or not fit for road use, and includes any chassis or body with or without wheels, appearing to have formed part of such a vehicle and any load carried by, and anything attached to, such a vehicle; AND any caravan, which means any structure designed or adapted for human habitation, capable of being moved from one place to another by towing or being transported on a motor vehicle or trailer and any motor vehicle so designed or adapted (but not a tent or railway rolling stock).

10. PROCURING DISCLOSURE OF COMPUTER-HELD PERSONAL DATA

Section 5(6) Data Protection Act 1984 (as amended by the Data Protection Act 1994 section 161)

(A) POINTS TO PROVE
1. That you 2. procured the disclosure to yourself
3. of personal data 4. the disclosure of which to you contravened subsection (2) or (3) of this section 5. knowing or having reason to believe that the disclosure constitutes such a contravention.

(B) MEANING OF TERMS
■ 1. 'That you'
Means the identity of the person who procured the disclosure.
■ 2. 'procured the disclosure to yourself'
Means to obtain, to get by some means or effort the information for himself.
■ 3. 'of personal data'
Defined as data consisting of information which related to a living

individual who can be identified from that information (or from that and other information in the possession of the data user), including any expression of opinion about the individual but not any indication of the intentions of the data user in respect of that individual. Therefore such information as a vehicle registration number, a national health number or a bank account number would be 'personal data' as the individual could be identifiable from other information in the possession of the data user.

A name and address is probably the most common form of 'personal data'. An example of 'opinion' and 'intentions' would be where a personnel manager has entered on the personal computer records of Smith that in his opinion Smith is ready for promotion and it is his intention to promote him to head of overseas sales. Here the 'opinion' is 'personal data' but the 'intentions' are not.

■ 4. 'the disclosure of which to you contravened subsection (2) or (3) of this section'

This means that such a disclosure was contrary to subsection (2) and (3) of section 5 viz:

(2) A person in respect of whom such an entry is contained in the register shall not:

(a) hold personal data of any description other than that speci-fied in the entry;

(b) hold any such data, or use any such data held by him, for any purpose other than the purpose or purposes described in the entry;

(c) obtain such data, or information to be contained in such data, to be held by him from any source which is not described in the entry;

(d) disclose such data held by him to any person who is not described in the entry; or

(e) directly or indirectly transfer such data held by him to any country or territory outside the United Kingdom other than one named or described in the entry.

(3) A servant or agent of a person to whom subsection (2) above applies shall, as respects personal data held by that person, be subject to the same restrictions on the use, disclosure or transfer of the data as those to which that person is subject under paragraphs (b), (c) and (e) of that subsection and, as respects personal data to be held by that person, to the same restrictions as those to which he is subject under paragraph (c) of that subsection.

The register mentioned in subsection (2) is the record kept by the Data Protection Registrar and a person shall not hold 'personal data' unless an entry in respect of that person as a data user is made in the register. To contravene subsections (2) and (3) the offender must act knowingly or recklessly.

■ **5. 'knowing or having reason to believe that the disclosure constitutes such a contravention'.**

Means that the offender or procurer must have guilty knowledge or at least suspect that the disclosure is an offence. For example if the computer operator tells the offender that it is an offence to make such a disclosure, then this would be good evidence of guilty knowledge. Where the offender has tried and failed to obtain the required information because he was not a registered disclosee he could have a reason to believe that such disclosure is an offence.

(C) USUAL METHODS OF PROVING THESE POINTS

■ **1. 'That you'**

Is normally proved by identifying the offender during the police interview.

■ **2. 'procured the disclosure to yourself'**

Can be proved by questions to the offender as to what he did to obtain the 'personal data' ie, did he make a straightforward request or did he pay money or use some other method to induce the computer operator to divulge the offending data. Similarly the computer operator could be asked to explain in a statement what the offender did or if the operator has committed offences as well, the police interview evidence could be of use.

■ 3. 'of personal data'

The information procured must fall into the definition of 'personal data', ie must relate to a living individual who can be identified from that information.

A description of the data in the police officer's statement of evidence showing how it relates to a living individual and how the individual can be identified from that information should suffice.

A printout of the personal data could be entered as an exhibit via the officer's statement and the statement of the computer operator. The case where a number or code relates to an individual but does not easily lead to the identity will cause problems, but it will be a question of fact for the court to decide whether such numbers amount to 'personal data'.

■ 4. 'the disclosure of which to you contravened subsections (2) or (3) of this section'

This could be put to the offender during the police interview that for example subsection (2)(d) was contravened, to wit, that the data user, Mrs Gisela Jones, disclosed personal data to Derek Taylor who was not described in the Data Protection Register as a disclosee.

■ 5. 'knowing or having reason to believe that the disclosure constitutes such a contravention'.

This would be best proved from the mouth of the offender during the police interview. Difficulties often arise when the state of a person's mind has to be proved. Failing an admission as to guilty knowledge a witness could be available to show that the offender had a reason to believe disclosure was such a contravention.

(D) SUPPORTING EVIDENCE

The admissibility in evidence of computer printouts was discussed in *R v Spiby* (1990) 91 Cr App R 186. Before a statement from a computer can be admissible in evidence it must be shown that the information has been recorded by mechanical means without the intervention of a human mind and the machine is reliable (which is usually presumed unless there is evidence to the contrary) and operating. A certificate to this effect giving the particulars prescribed in section 69 of the Police and Criminal Evidence Act 1984 must be produced.

Formerly, procuring disclosure, eg by deception, was a grey area but now section 161 of the Criminal Justice and Public Order Act 1994 puts the matter beyond doubt by adding the new offence, at section 5(6) of the Data Protection Act.

Note 1. Certain exemptions apply to this offence under Part IV Data Protection Act 1984 such as for national security.
Note 2. Subsections (7) and (8) of the Data Protection Act create the offences of selling and offering to sell, respectively, such information.
Note 3 section 10 of the Computer Misuse Act 1990 which allows an enforcement officer (which includes a constable) to have access to computer material.
Note 4. See offence 16(B)3, Criminal damage, for computer hacking and impairing the proper use of a computer.

11. TICKET TOUT OFFENCE
Section 166 Criminal Justice and Public Order Act 1994

(A) POINTS TO PROVE
1. That you, 2. being an unauthorised person 3. did sell, or offer or expose for sale, 4. a ticket for a designated football match, namely .... 5. in any public place or place to which the public has access or 6. in the course of a trade or business, in any other place.

(B) MEANING OF TERMS

■ 1. 'That you'

Means the identity of the ticket tout.

■ 2. 'being an unauthorised person'

This is defined as 'a person is "unauthorised" unless he is authorised in writing to sell tickets for the match by the home club or by the organisers of the match'.

■ 3. 'did sell, or offer or expose for sale'

The normal places for touts are outside the ground in question before the game or alongside the queues waiting for tickets. Sale etc will be obvious from the actions of the tout and his customers. Money should normally change hands for a sale or the tout's sales patter will show an offering or exposing for sale.

In theory an exposing for sale could be committed by merely showing the tickets to prospective customers, although words or an actual sale would normally be easier to prove.

■ 4. 'a ticket for a designated football match, namely ....'

'Ticket' is defined as anything which purports to be a ticket. 'Designated football match' is defined as a football match, or football match of a description, for the time being designated under section 1(1) of the Football (Offences) Act 1991. The particular football match should be shown.

■ 5. 'in any public place or place to which the public has access'

Usual places for this offence will be on the street or in public houses or clubs. In the absence of a judicial decision it is considered that a place will still be public even if admission is on payment, eg an outdoor pop concert, agricultural show or point-to-point meeting.

■ 6. 'in the course of a trade or business ....'.

This phrase means that where the tout sells etc in the course of a trade or business then the offence can be committed anywhere, such as in the privacy of a dwelling house.

(C) USUAL METHODS OF PROVING THESE POINTS

■ 1. 'That you'

This is proved by the officer dealing with the offence, eg, 'I saw a man, I now know to be Ashley Jackson, in Elland Road, Leeds outside Leeds United Football Club . . . ' The reasons for knowing Ashley Jackson would be from his car, by examining his driving licence, passport or visiting his house or talking to his neighbours or a combination of those or other similar things. In difficult cases it should be borne in mind that the offence is an arrestable offence.

■ 2. 'being an unauthorised person'

This point can be proved by asking the suspect, 'Have you any authority or permission to sell those tickets?'

This could be backed up by taking statements from the home club or the match organisers to show they hadn't given written permission as required by the Act.

■ 3.'did sell, or offer or expose for sale'

These verbs can be proved by observations of a plain clothes officer who could say in his statement that he saw money change hands, the tout walking up and down the queue of football supporters shouting out his prices or merely showing a selection of tickets in his hand to the persons in the queue.

Further evidence could be obtained by taking statements from persons in the queue.

■ 4. 'a ticket for a designated football match, namely ....'

The 'ticket' can be seized for evidence whether it is an actual ticket or a forgery and shown an an exhibit in the officer's statement of evidence.

As this offence is an arrestable offence, note that the consequent police power of search and entry will include a vehicle reasonably believed to be used in the offence. A football match can be proved to be designated by referring to the Football (Offences) Act 1991.

■ **5. 'in any public place or place to which the public had access'**

The proof of this point can be made by the officer in the case describing the place, eg, 'In High Street outside the Craig Thompson Ticket Agents Office'. In cases where doubt exists, such as the foyer of the ticket office, statements from the owner or occupier of the premises would be beneficial.

■ **6. 'in the course of a trade or business in any other place'.**

It would be necessary to show the tout was running a trade or business. If this is denied by the tout, such things as advertising in local papers, shop windows, letter heads or business cards, telephone company records and tax returns or VAT registration might help prove this point. Once it is proved that the tout is trading then any other place is included.

(D) SUPPORTING EVIDENCE

Note. The Home Secretary has power in this section for the discretionary making of an order to extend this offence to sporting events for which 6,000 or more tickets are issued for sale.

12. TAXI TOUT OFFENCE

Section 167 Criminal Justice and Public Order Act 1994

(A) POINTS TO PROVE

1. That you 2. did solicit persons 3. in a public place, namely .... 4. to hire vehicles 5. to carry them as passengers.

(B) MEANING OF TERMS

■ **1. 'That you'**

Means the identity of the person soliciting.

■ 2. 'did solicit persons'
Means to incite or induce persons. The mere display of a sign on a vehicle that the vehicle is for hire does not amount to soliciting.

■ 3. 'in a public place'
Means any highway and 'any other premises or place to which at the material time the public have or are permitted to have access (whether on payment or otherwise)'.

■ 4. 'to hire vehicles'
Means a borrowing for a price. Borrowing is normally free but a borrowing for money or other consideration is a contract of hire. 'Vehicle' is defined in the glossary ante.

■ 5. 'to carry them as passengers'.
This phrase means to transport a person or persons from A to B. However, as the offence we are dealing with is complete with the mere soliciting, there is no need for an actual hiring or carrying of passenger.

(C) USUAL METHODS OF PROVING THESE POINTS
■ 1. 'That you'
Usually proved by the officer who witnessed the soliciting/touting.

■ 2. 'did solicit persons'
This point can be proved by admission during interview and/or from what the witnesses saw. The offender might give out business cards, display leaflets, talk to people waiting for legitimate taxis or drive around in a vehicle inciting or encouraging people to hire him for a lift home etc. Any printed or written word used by the offender should be seized for evidence and appear as an exhibit in the police officer's statement.

■ 3. 'in a public place, namely ....'
This point is normally proved by naming the street in the officer's statement. When difficulty is foreseen, such as private premises where for that day the public have access on payment of £5 each, then a statement from an organiser of the event may be necessary.

■ 4. 'to hire vehicles'

Can be proved from what the offender said or displayed during the 'soliciting' eg, 'We'll take you for half the taxi fare' or, 'We aren't more expensive after midnight'.

Note that some money or consideration must be mentioned or implied in the inciting.

■ 5. 'to carry them as passengers'.

This phrase, like the previous one, is proved from what the offender says or displays during the soliciting. Admissions during the police interview or from what witnesses to the incitement heard the defendant say or saw him do are the usual ways of proving this point.

(D) SUPPORTING EVIDENCE

If the soliciting is in pursuance of a special shared taxi scheme under the Transport Act 1985, then the above offence does not apply. It is a defence to show that the soliciting was for passengers for public services vehicles on behalf of the holder of a PSV operator's licence and with that person's authority. This offence is an arrestable offence under the Police and Criminal Evidence Act 1984, section 24(2).

13. POACHING AT NIGHT

Section 1 Night Poaching Act 1828

(A) POINTS TO PROVE

1. That you 2. did by night 3. unlawfully enter (or be on land), whether open or enclosed 4. with a gun (net, engine, or other instrument) 5. for the purpose of taking or destroying 6. game.

(B) MEANING OF TERMS

■ 1. 'That you' Means the identity of the poacher.

■ 2. 'did by night'

'Night' is defined as commencing at the expiration of the first hour after sunset and concluding at the beginning of the last hour before sunrise.

■ 3. 'unlawfully enter (or be on) land whether open or enclosed'

This point means a personal entry as opposed to a constructive entry by the poacher's dog. Open land appears to be land without hedges, walls or fences and enclosed land would appear to have some means of enclosure.

■ 4. 'with a gun (net, engine, or other instrument)'

Note that a dog is not included, therefore a person who enters land for the purpose of taking game with a dog does not commit this offence (unless he also has a gun, net, engine or other instrument). If he is successful with the dog alone and takes game he would commit the offence of taking game by night, also contrary to section 1 Night Poaching Act 1828.

■ 5. 'for the purpose of taking or destroying'

This means that the purpose for him being on the land is the taking alive or killing of the game.

■ 6. 'game'.

'Game' is defined as hares, pheasants, partridges, grouse, heath or moor game, black game and bustards. Note that rabbits are not game' under this Act, ie they are included in the offence of actually taking game (or rabbits) but are not included in the merely 'entering on land' offence.

(C) USUAL METHODS OF PROVING THESE POINTS

■ 1. 'That you'

This point will probably be proved by the witness who found the poacher, eg the gamekeeper.

■ 2. 'did by night'

This can be proved in the police officer's statement coupled with the witness who actually saw what time the poacher was entering onto the land. Sunrise and sunset should be proved. Where there is any doubt a court can take judicial notice of such times by consulting an almanac.

■ **3. 'unlawfully enter (or be on) land whether open or enclosed.'**
This point can be proved by the gamekeeper or other witness to the personal entry on to the land by the poacher. A brief description of the land may help the court, ie whether open or enclosed.

■ **4. 'with a gun (net, engine or other instrument)'**
Again the observations of the witnesses will prove this point together with any item seized for evidence.

■ **5. 'for the purpose of taking or destroying'**
Only the purpose needs proving not the actual taking of game. This is in the mind of the poacher or his accomplices. It will usually be proved by admission from the poacher, but circumstantial evidence may be adequate to show a purpose (or intent) to take or destroy game. Eg possessing all the necessary equipment.

■ **6. 'game'.**
Occasionally an expert witness may be needed to identify the particular game, but in the vast majority of cases a statement from a witness or police officer will prove this point.

14. RAVE OFFENCE
Section 63 Criminal Justice and Public Order Act 1994

(A) POINTS TO PROVE
1. That you 2. knowing that a direction had been given that applied to you 3. failed to leave land as soon as reasonably practicable 4. when a rave was in progress (or in preparation).

(B) MEANING OF TERMS
■ **1. 'That you'**
Means the person to whom the direction has been given.

■ 2. 'knowing that a direction had been given that applied to you'

This point is explained at section 63(2) of the CJPO Act as follows. If, as respects any land in the open air, a police officer of at least the rank of superintendent reasonably believes that:

(a) two or more persons are making preparations for the holding there of a gathering to which this section applies,

(b) 10 or more persons are waiting for such a gathering to begin there, or

(c) 10 or more persons are attending such a gathering which is in progress;

he may give a direction that those persons and any other persons who come to prepare or wait for or to attend the gathering are to leave the land and remove any vehicles or other property which they have with them on the land.

If the superintendent does not communicate with all the 'ravers' any constable at the scene may pass on the direction.

To help in proving the mental element of 'knowing', section 63(4) provides that: 'persons shall be treated as having had a direction communicated to them if reasonable steps have been taken to bring it to their attention.'

Therefore any loudhailer broadcast would appear to be a reasonable step.

Note that this direction also applies to vehicles and property eg, amplifiers, speakers, tents, caravans etc.

■ 3. 'failed to leave land as soon as reasonably practicable'

Means that the person(s) who have had the direction communicated to them should move off the land together with any of their property. 'Reasonably practicable' would allow for common sense to prevail where invalids, the old or very young or large amounts of equipment etc are present.

The land must be 'land in the open air' which includes a place partly open to the air, eg a dutch barn (basically a roof supported by four posts).

Persons exempt from leaving the land are the occupier, his family or employees or agents and any person whose home is situated on the land.

A defence exists for failing to leave the land as soon as practicable where the accused can show he had a reasonable excuse, eg illness or injury or possibly the loss of some valuable object etc.

■ 4. 'when a rave was in progress (or in preparation)'

'Rave' is defined in section 63(1) of the Act:

This section applies to a gathering on land in the open air of 100 or more persons (whether or not trespassers) at which amplified music is played during the night (with or without intermissions) and is such as, by reason of its loudness and duration and the time at which it is played, is likely to cause serious distress to the inhabitants of the locality; and for this purpose –

(a) such a gathering continues during intermissions in the music and, where the gathering extends over several days, throughout the period during which amplified music is played at night (with or without intermissions); and

(b) 'music' includes sounds wholly or predominantly characterised by the emission of a succession of repetitive beats.

Once it is considered that such a rave is being planned, the direction can be given to 'nip it in the bud' at the preparation stage or the stage where only ten or more people are present.

(C) USUAL METHODS OF PROVING THESE POINTS

■ 1. 'That you'

This point will be proved by the officer in the case either arresting the offender or identifying him for process by summons.

■ 2. 'knowing that a direction had been given that applied to you'

An admission from the accused that he knew a direction had been given and that it applied to him would be best evidence. Failing that the officer should prove that 'reasonable steps had been taken to bring it to their attention', eg an explanation in his statement of what he had said to the accused or a statement from the superintendent who had given the original direction.

■ **3. 'failed to leave land as soon as reasonably practicable'**
This point could be proved by the officer showing the time of the direction and the fact that some time later the accused was still on the land and taking no steps to leave. The two defences should be borne in mind and questions asked if in doubt, eg, 'Do you or your family live or work on this land?' or 'Have you any reasonable excuse for not leaving this land?'

A description of the land in question should be made in the police officer's statement to prove it was 'land in the open air.'

■ **4. 'when a rave is in progress (or in preparation)'.**
The police must prove that the 'gathering' or rave comes within the definition at (B)4 ante. This is easily done when such a gathering is in progress. If it is only in preparation, the superintendent would have to prove that he 'reasonably believed' that the gathering would come under section 63.

(D) SUPPORTING EVIDENCE

Note 1. This offence also caters for those who return to the land within a period of seven days beginning with the day on which the direction was given (unless they can show a reasonable excuse for again entering the land).

Note 2. There is a power of arrest without warrant for a constable in uniform, who reasonably suspects an offence under section 63 has been committed. Supplementary powers of entry and seizure are provided in section 64 of the Act. Section 65 provides a power to stop persons from proceeding to raves where a direction under section 63 has been given.

Note 3. All the above only applies to 'land in the open air' and not to premises, buildings, clubs etc.

the New Police Bookshop

Points to Prove	£13.00

Fifth ed March 2000, Stewart Calligan   ISBN 0 9533058 9 9
is published by The New Police Bookshop (East Yorkshire)

From the same publisher

The Custody Officer's Companion   £16.50
revised 2nd ed 1998, Stewart Calligan & Paul Harper   ISBN 0 9533058 0 5

Policing Your Health   £10.00
first ed 1999, Stewart Calligan & Alan Charlesworth   ISBN 0 9533058 8 0

To order any of the three NPB (E Yorks) titles, write to Stewart Calligan,
The New Police Bookshop (East Yorkshire) PO Box 124, Goole DN14 7FH
Cheques should be made payable to the New Police Bookshop

From The New Police Bookshop (Surrey)

Agricultural Vehicles on the Road: a guide to the legislation   £12.50
first ed 2000, Andrew McMahon   ISBN 0 9533058 7 2

The Special Constable's Manual   £17.85
revised second ed 1999, Tom Barron   ISBN 0 9533058 6 4

The Child Protection Investigators' Companion   £12.50
second ed 1999, Kevin Smith   ISBN 0 9533058 3 X

Investigative Interviewing Explained   £12.50
first ed 1999, Brian Ord and Gary Shaw   ISBN 0 9533058 2 1

Crime Patrol: to recognise and arrest criminals   £12.50
first ed 1998, Mike McBride   ISBN 0 9533058 1 3

The Human Factor: maximising the use of police informants   £14.50
first ed 2000, Tim Roberts   ISBN 0 9533058 4 8

Police Powers: a practitioner's guide   £12.50
first ed 2000, Allan Greaves and David Pickover   ISBN 0 9533058 5 6

To order NPB (Surrey) titles, Tel: 0117 9555 215 Fax 0117 9541 485
Email npb@brookland-mailing.co.uk
Alternatively write to NPB, Brookland Mailing Services, Unit 4,
Parkway Trading Estate, St Werburghs Road, Bristol BS2 9PG.
Cheques should be made payable to the New Police Bookshop.